Entrepreneurs
The Secrets to Thriving in Uncertain Times
(EXPANDED EDITION)

Brian Schwartz

WISE
MEDIA GROUP

50 Interviews: Entrepreneurs
Copyright © 2009 by Brian Schwartz
www.50interviews.com

Library of Congress Control Number: 2009923062

Published by
Wise Media Group
444 17th Street, Suite 507
Denver, CO 80202

Expanded edition.
Printed in the United States of America.

This book is dedicated to all the entrepreneurs in the world working hard to make a difference, and who serve as examples that only by taking risks will we ever live life to the fullest. You are true role models who inspire many of us through your actions.

To my family, friends, and teachers who I've always admired, and have given me strength to carry on when I needed it most. To my past coworkers who stood up for me, and the employers who empowered us along the way.

To those who have already listened to me share my passion, and to those of you who soon will. More importantly, to those of you who catch the spark. Through this endeavor, it's been reaffirmed time and time again that the more we share, the more we become. In being truly open to each other's views, we accept the truth that we know far less than we think we do.

Praise for 50 Interviews: Entrepreneurs

"Whether you are thinking about starting a business or already have, *50 Interviews* shows that you don't need to make all the mistakes yourself, Read this book and learn from those who are already succeeding. Quit dreaming and start living."

Joe Sabah, Founding President of the Colorado Speakers Association

"Very few books these days combine short vignettes with powerful direct impacts that can be used immediately. The return on investment for *50 Interviews* is two minutes tops. Brian's formulaic approach enables the reader to extract the collective insight and experience of 50 divergent entrepreneurs. His dialogue throughout the book allows us to vicariously ask the questions we would have wanted to ask any successful entrepreneur and learn succinctly what worked for them."

Michael R. Webb, Co-Founder, Aubice LLC

"*50 Interviews* is a must-have for any serious entrepreneur. As a successful author, writer's coach and part-owner of a small press, I can attest to the pure satisfaction of creating and running a business you love, but also the myriad challenges. One of the characteristics of true entrepreneurs, though, is that we never stop learning, and reading Brian Schwartz's interviews has given me new insights and inspiration. I've been reading an interview a day to spark my creative energy and focus on the expert advice from each business owner. This book is great not just for those considering entrepreneurship, but for those of us living the dream."

Teresa R. Funke, Author of "Remember Wake,"
"Dancing in Combat Boots" and The Home-Front Heroes Collection

"*50 Interviews* provides fifty unique perspectives in how to be successful, fulfilled and the best at what you do."

Joel Garfinkle, Founder of www.dreamjobcoaching.com

"There are two ways to learn about entrepreneurship: one, give it a try, and two, talk to people who have lived and breathed it for years in the crucibles of start-ups. *50 Interviews* gives readers a front-row seat to the action, offering future entrepreneurs lessons learned the hard way. Read it, learn, and then go do it!"

Gregg Vanourek, Founding partner, New Mountain Ventures, and co-author, Life Entrepreneurs: Ordinary People Creating Extraordinary Lives

"The vast majority of "entrepreneurship" experts in the world tell you what you want to hear. But in *50 interviews*, the interviewees tell you what you need to hear. It is an eye opening and must read book if you want to know the cold hard truth about true entrepreneurship."

Jerèll Klaver, Founder of SALUS® Customize your Bath and Body Care

ACKNOWLEDGEMENTS

I never could have imagined the immense effort involved in writing a book such as this. It simply would never have been possible without the generosity of others who thankfully share the passion I do for this project.

To the 50+ entrepreneurs who graciously provided their valuable time to participate in the interview itself, I dedicate the end result to you and know that your stories will inspire and move others towards a direction of true fulfillment and greater contribution.

I owe a debt of gratitude to Landmark Education and all the committed volunteers and staff members, especially Pam Valvano and Dani Zerbib, in the Denver and Utah offices. They are making a remarkable impact in the world.

To my supportive wife and family who along with me didn't realize where this was going when it started, but have been there for me through it all.

An amazing group of truly extraordinary givers, for without their contribution, this project would have never evolved to the point it has; Andy Piszkin, Carrie Pinsky, Maryann Swartz, Braun Mincher, Rob McNealy, Bob McDonnell, Chad Cameron and Isaac Allen (The Leap! Guys), Deb Frey, Nick Zelinger, Kerrie Flanagan, Peter Olins, Patrick Gill, Doug Johnson, and David Cunningham.

To the other writers who graciously contributed valuable content for the appendices listed at the end of the book; Tom Frey, Dave Block, Larry Nelson, Erin Duckhorn, Ken Munsch, and Bob Parsons.

Most notably Veronica Yager, an amazing force. Who inspired me with a work ethic rarely seen, and took this project further than I ever envisioned, I often find myself in awe of what has evolved! There is no doubt that you will go far in this life and reach a level of success others will aspire to.

A genuine thank you in advance to the many individuals and organizations that will be so pivotal after the completion of this first book, for now I'm learning that the real work begins.

There are countless more organizations and individuals that although I may not have mentioned you here, know that I am grateful to each of you, and that you each made a difference.

Brian Schwartz
Fort Collins, Colorado

FOREWORD

I first met Brian Schwartz in May of 2008, when he wanted to talk with me about a project he was calling 50 Entrepreneurs. When we met, I saw a lot of energy in Brian. It was the energy of curiosity. Brian was interviewing 50 entrepreneurs in order to learn more about entrepreneurship. The ironic thing was Brian was not an entrepreneur himself.

During the interview, Brian and I discussed my career history and transition from full-time employee to full-time entrepreneur. He was very interested in entrepreneurship. We talked about many of the other interviews he had done, and what he planned to do with the interviews when he was finished.

I really loved what Brian was trying to do, so I gave him some introductions along the way, and tried to help him with his project where I could. Over time, Brian and I became friends. Brian has also changed a lot since we first met. During the course of his project, Brian started down his own path toward becoming an entrepreneur.

Fast forwarding to today, Brian Schwartz is a much different person. Brian changed the direction of the 50 Entrepreneurs project, to a much larger 50 Interviews™ business. Brian took the leap; he is now an entrepreneur himself. He is more confident, energized, and most importantly, happier, now that he is building his own entrepreneurial dream, rather than someone else's.

The transformation that Brian went through, from employee to entrepreneur, is an amazing journey I have witnessed many times before through my work in the small business and startup communities. I've also undergone the transition myself. It is a very life-altering journey and I think that Brian has devised the most amazing system to make the transition as smooth as possible.

Recent studies suggest that more than 80 percent of all businesses fail within the first five years. That is a staggering number, and there are many reasons why this occurs. Often times, people don't have great mentors and industry contacts to guide them around land mines. They choose to start businesses in fields which they simply don't have a chance. New entrepreneurs often repeat mistakes that many others have made before them. Sadly, many people can't recover from these mistakes and their businesses fail.

What I can confidently say is that Brian Schwartz has come up with a way to improve your odds at success, save you thousands, if not tens of thousands of dollars, and jump-start your project or business by years, by gaining great insight and industry connections in any field in which you want to start a business or project in.

I highly recommend this book, and you will not believe how easy and powerful the 50 Interviews™ system is. What you find in the following pages will permanently change your life in the most profound ways.

Rob McNealy

TABLE OF CONTENTS

"All truth passes through three stages. First, it is ridiculed. Second, it is violently opposed. Third, it is accepted as being self-evident."

- Arthur Schopenhauer

INTRODUCTION

When I first began the interview process, my intention was simply to explore the possibilities of entrepreneurship to see if it was the path for me. I wanted to take a look at what being in business for myself really meant before I took the leap. I must give credit where credit is due. It was my wise and wonderful wife, Debi, who suggested I interview 50 entrepreneurs. She secretly hoped that by the time I interviewed 50 people, I would forget about this crazy idea and stick to my daily grind. Truthfully, we were both pretty fearful of giving up the security of a steady paycheck to start a business.

I took my wife's advice and began reaching out to schedule interviews with entrepreneurs from a variety of industries and backgrounds. What began as a career exploration exercise turned into something much bigger than I ever imagined. In the process of doing those first 50 interviews, I had a personal awakening. I was enlightened, not only about all things entrepreneurial, but also about the power of the interview process itself. I am a voracious reader of non-fiction. I have always enjoyed learning from the experiences of others. As I completed each interview, I was struck by the potency of the information that was being offered through the oral exchange of ideas.

When information is shared orally and in the first person, the truth, in all its glory, comes out. When we write, we can't help but make little corrections. As we strive to conform grammatically, socially or culturally to prescribed conventions, the essence of our story is often diluted. Bits of truth remain but important aspects of the message get lost in the translation as we put our thoughts and oral musings into written form.

By taking the time to ask questions of people who are living some reality and then really listening to the answers, I discovered the unwritten rules, the unspoken truths and particular insights of the entrepreneurial experience. I was given the opportunity to stand, for a moment, in fifty different pairs of shoes of people actually in the trenches of the experience. The interviews are unedited and unadulterated by the filters of well-meaning writers and editors, or even by the entrepreneurs themselves. This gives readers the opportunity to discern the information in its purest form and to ultimately draw their own conclusions.

As a result of doing 50 interviews, I did make the leap from employee to entrepreneur. My career exploration ultimately became the catalyst for a vibrant business enterprise involving many different people. Hundreds of other 50 Interview© titles are currently in the process of being developed and published as a series. Exploring 50 different perspectives on a single topic is transformative and it is exciting to see the concept applied to so many different life experiences.

In the interviews that follow, you will discover some unexpected truths. I invite you to open your mind, set any preconceived notions aside and step into someone else's shoes. The hope is that through the process of learning from the experiences of others, you will be inspired to take action and move forward on your own journey.

1

"If you don't have a plan, someone will have one for you."
Paul Anderson, Paul L. Anderson Productions, Inc.

◆

BACKGROUND

Paul Anderson started Paul L. Anderson Productions, *www.paulanderson.com,* in 1982. He has two employees and is based in Fort Collins, Colorado. Major clients include Hewlett-Packard, Intel, Waterpik, Agilent, and Philips Medical. Paul came from an educational background (he was a professor at a university) and prior to his current company, he had no experience as an entrepreneur. Paul's initial investment was $10,000 which he borrowed from the bank and used the funds to purchase equipment and build a photographic studio.

INTERVIEW

Q: Did you use a business plan?

A: Not a specific plan...but built into my model was to always adapt to the needs of my clients and deliver a high quality product. Thus, my business moved over time from a commercial photographic studio to a multi-media/video production company.

Q: The genesis of the idea?

A: It was in my second year sabbatical at Colorado State University that I began to really embrace my love for photography. I spent three years working with another studio before striking off on my own. I credit much of my courage to leave the security as a tenured professor to my supportive wife, being young and naïve and perhaps a bit of blind enthusiasm.

Q: Is there a passion that this fills for you personally?

A: I am very passionate about being creative. I was inspired early on by pioneers of photography like Ansel Adams, Weston, and Stiglitz. My job is an outlet for self-expression and I continually get inspired by creating something from nothing.

Q: Where do you see yourself and your company in 10 years?

A: Being age 64 now...retired, with the possibility of handing over the majority of ownership to an apprentice. I would like to stay involved in the business.

Q: Looking back now, is there anything you wish you had done differently? What do you know now that you wish you'd known sooner?

A: Pricing/Value – the importance of establishing what you are worth and what jobs you are willing to take. There are a lot of low paying jobs out there and you need to be willing to walk away from them – after all, isn't that why you go into business for yourself in the first place? You've got to determine early on your worth. **Growth** – I owe much of my success to my ability to partner with other contractors/vendors. I could have hired several people for the work we do, but have found that partnering with other companies and individuals has worked out very well. Give them ownership in the final product and they will add great value to your work. **Self promotion** – you need to be able to market yourself well and not be too humble. Give a client what they need, not what they want. Listening to what they need is key. They may tell you they want one thing, but what they really need is formed in your listening to them.

> *"Give a client what they need, not what they want. Listening to what they need is key."*

Q: What have been your biggest rewards?

A: A sense of accomplishment that my work made a real difference in the success of a company's product. Getting past the fear factor and seeing results that far exceed even my own expectations at times.

Q: Are there one or two things you can attribute your success to? Luck, timing, someone who helped you?

A: At the start of my days as an entrepreneur, I entered my work

PAUL L. ANDERSON PRODUCTIONS, INC.

into a contest. Although I didn't win any awards, the production aspects of my submission impressed the group that sponsored the event. A few months later one of the attendees called the sponsoring group and asked if they knew anyone who did top notch slide shows. They suggested my company, and from that referral, I got my first big client who provided plenty of work over the years. I actually attribute my success to two major setbacks I experienced. Although I didn't know it at the time, they turned out to be blessings in disguise. My number one client, my sugar daddy, terminated our contract due to budget cuts and my number one go to vendor/partner was no longer able to do work for me. These two events while difficult to deal with at the time, forced me to diversify my business

> *"I actually attribute my success to two major setbacks I experienced. Although I didn't know it at the time, they turned out to be blessings in disguise."*

and pursue new projects/clients and expand my network of partners who all brought more creativity and ideas which really helped my business thrive.

Q: How do you attract and retain the best employees? What is the most important attribute you look for?

A: I am a big proponent of using contractors in lieu of hiring employees.

Q: Recommended training and resources? Do you recommend an MBA?

A: No on the MBA. Suggested reading: *The HP Way* by David Packard. I suggest that you seek out inspiration and the work of those you admire. Whenever possible, surround yourself with the best and learn from them; don't be intimated by them.

Q: Slogan to live by or what it might say on your tombstone?

A: "You've got to suffer." Notably because the real lean years in the beginning have proved so valuable. "Make outrageous connections" (for creativity). This is the one thing that I have

PAUL ANDERSON

built my reputation on. "If you don't have a plan, someone will have one for you." This goes back to the moment I declared that if this life was going to ever be of my choice, I would have to start making decisions, or someone else would.

PAUL's TIPS FROM THE TRENCHES

1. Find good people.

2. Never saying no to an opportunity and being willing to try anything. Throw your hat into the ring.

3. Just put yourself out there. Don't let fear of failure dissuade you from trying something new.

4. Find a sugar daddy (top account) to live on for a-while.

PAUL L. ANDERSON PRODUCTIONS, INC.

"He had a lot of fun!"
Michael Burns, Burns Marketing

◆

BACKGROUND

Michael Burns established his Loveland, Colorado communications company, Burns Marketing, in 1972 when he was 24. He had no prior entrepreneur experience, and had been working as a writer for Epsilon Sigma Alpha International. He was inspired to start his business by Leon Fedderson, who had purchased the historic Stanley Hotel in Estes Park, Colorado, and needed a writer to help him market it. Besides becoming his first client, Leon instilled in him the belief that "anything is possible." His company mantra is "To be Relentless, Insightful, and Creative." Michael attributes his company's successful thirty percent annual growth rate to his twenty six employees. He has not had to add significant staff, but rather has leveraged their talents and the technology available to them. He envisions Burns Marketing as a much larger entity in the future. To accomplish that, he is now partnering with other marketing companies around the world with the vision of providing a higher level of service to his clients.

INTERVIEW

Q: What was your initial startup cost and source?
A: $1000, bank loan.

Q: How long until there was a positive cash flow?
A: Immediate. I didn't start the business until I had a client.

Q: Did you use a business plan?
A: No

Q: What was the genesis of the idea?
A: My first client drove me to start the business in the first place.

MICHAEL BURNS

Leon Fedderson purchased the historic Stanley Hotel in Estes Park, Colorado, and needed a writer to help him market it.

Q: What is the vision of the company and the community you serve? What came first, the problem or the solution?

A: The need is there. We strive to be the best marketing communications company in Colorado while serving clients around the world. Our company mantra is "To be Relentless, Insightful, and Creative," and to do whatever it takes to make our clients successful. We follow a proven methodology which involves a fair amount of research before we begin the creativity phase. We are constantly seeking cutting edge technology, and exploring new techniques.

Q: What is the passion that it fills for you personally?

A: Everyday is different! It's fulfilling to be in the middle of the most positive, exciting, and creative time for a company, when they are launching a new product or themselves. Everyday we are building something new, and working with clients who are moving their solutions forward.

> *"Our company mantra is to be Relentless, Insightful, and Creative, and to do whatever it takes to make our clients successful."*

Q: Where do you see yourself and your company in 10 years?

A: I envision Burns Marketing as a much larger entity. We've been growing at a rate of thirty percent a year. Amazingly, this growth has come without adding significant staff, but rather leveraging the talents and the technology available to us.

Q: What were your biggest challenges? Looking back now, is there anything you wish you had done differently?

A: People; finding the right combination of talent and youth. We don't micromanage our employees. You have to be self driven and self directed. Our culture is very entrepreneur-centric. We encourage risk taking as long as you learn from your mistakes and adjust accordingly. Another challenge has been technology and techniques. Marketing is a fast evolv-

BURNS MARKETING

ing industry. A phenomenon like "viral marketing" requires us to change our approach, and try new things. We have to remain agile to be successful.

Q: What aspects of ownership are the most rewarding? Were there any unexpected rewards?

A: Seeing our employees grow. We typically hire younger employees, and it is rewarding to see them develop. I'd have to say the financial aspect has been the biggest unexpected reward.

Q: Are there one or two things you can attribute your success to? Was it luck, timing, someone who helped you?

A: Our employees without a doubt. Burns Marketing is where it is today because of the people who work for us. Two hires in particular took the companies to heights I never could have imagined. Leon inspired me at a young age. He instilled in me the belief that "anything is possible." Another successful attribute is being open to new approaches, new ideas, and challenging the status quo. One example of this is that we recently joined TAAN, (Transworld Advertising Agency Network). We are now partnering with other marketing companies around the world with a shared vision of providing a higher level of service to our client.

Q: How do you attract and retain the best employees? What is the most important attribute you look for?

A: We seek out people who are driven, self-starters, and who are willing to make mistakes, but then learn from them. We don't supervise people here, and I guess that leads to a very entrepreneurial-like environment. I put the profits of the company back into the people. We encourage them to attend conferences and training, have an annual retreat every year, and the attractive surroundings we work in here were created to benefit all the employees who work in it.

> *"I am a firm believer that if you like what you are doing, the money will follow."*

MICHAEL BURNS

Q: Any good books that you recommend?

A: *Good to Great* by Jim Collins. It is the blueprint for our business, and *The One Minute Manager* by Kenneth H. Blanchard and Spencer Johnson.

Q: Do you recommend an MBA?

A: I have no opinion really because I don't have one myself.

Q: Slogan to live by or what it might say on your tombstone?

A: "He had a lot of fun!"

Q: Anything else you'd like to add?

A: On the element of passion: I am a firm believer that if you like what you are doing, the money will follow. I originally wanted to be a travel writer. In everything I've ever done, it has never been about the money.

Burns Marketing

"The world is an illusion, have fun!"
Chad Cameron, Leap Ventures

◆

BACKGROUND
Chad Cameron founded Leap Ventures LLC with business partner Isaac Allen in 2007 in Loveland, Colorado. They have three
employees and use several contractors as needed. Prior to Leap
Ventures, Chad was the owner of an information technology
services company for eight years which he sold in 2008. Similar to my own journey with this book, Leap Ventures emerged
for Chad and Isaac as a journey to self discovery, leading them
to a set of newfound truths and beliefs. In the process, they
discovered a way to live extraordinary lives that often eludes
the vast majority of us. After spending a significant amount of
time with Chad and Isaac, I attribute the peaceful positive state
which surrounds them as a new awareness that true freedom
and fulfillment, or enlightenment, can only occur by acting on
your inspired thoughts. Acting from inspiration means you have
to remove your filters and step out of your own way to let the
genuine, authentic expression of your true self shine through.
A large piece is leaving your ego behind. The more time I spend
around the *Leap Guys*, the more I feel at peace with the unpre-
dictability of the world in which we live. I highly recommend
their film, and more information on it can be found at the end
of this interview.

INTERVIEW
Q: What was your initial startup cost and source?
A: $100,000 from both a home equity loan and from cashing
out my entire Roth IRA and depleting all my savings.

Q. How long until you reached positive cash flow?
A: Not sure. I recently spoke with a peer in the business who
shared with me he was expecting to break even after 18

CHAD CAMERON

months on a $200k film, and I know many documentaries never break even, but it was never about the money. I suspect it really depends largely on the distribution of the film and right now we have a couple of opportunities that could really accelerate things. I can say we are paying our bills every month and that the money just shows up when we need it.

Q. Did you use a business plan?
A: No. What is a business plan?

Q. What was the genesis of the idea?
A: Isaac and I met in a community leadership program at Landmark Education. My project for the course was to create a short film where I interviewed several people who overcame serious disabilities to live extraordinary lives. I wanted to discover what was different about them. Why did they not give up with such daunting circumstances? What was their source of faith and energy? In March of 2006, impacted by Robert Scheinfeld's *Busting Loose from the Money Game*, I attended one of his seminars that expanded the concepts in his book, to see life in a much different, empowering way, unlike anything I had experienced before. An inspired thought emerged; "What if I talked to a group of people who had taken on living their lives according to this philosophy?" I thought what a great opportunity to interview people living a life 24/7 that I had only gotten occasionally glimpses of. Sharing an intense interest in this new philosophy, Isaac and I became close friends. He suggested we write a book about viewing the world as an illusion. I said that is a great idea but lets make a movie about it instead! We knew nothing about how to make a movie when we started. People told us we were crazy. We heard a lot about "how it is done." We learned how to do it as we went along. We made some mistakes and learned something new every day.

> *"To get some professional help in the very beginning might have helped us make fewer mistakes early on."*

LEAP VENTURES

Q. The vision of the company and the community you serve?

A: To live life from inspiration and create positive material to share with the world. In a world often viewed as problematic, we produce and promote only ideas, products and people that encourage and challenge each of us to explore our reality from a positive and empowering perspective.

Q. What is the passion that it fills for you personally?

A: This is fun for me. I get to surround myself with great people and live from a source of inspiration every day.

Q. Where do you see yourself and your company in 10 years?

A: I have no clue and I don't worry about it. I know it is out of my control anyway. I guess I just don't have any attachment to a specific outcome.

Q. Looking back now, is there anything you wish you had done differently?

A: We started out with some bad footage because we hired someone we thought was an expert who wasn't. To get some professional help in the very beginning might have helped us make fewer mistakes early on. I had an idea of what I thought it took to make a film, and the reality is far different than what I had envisioned. There is an amazing amount of work that goes into making a film that you will never understand until you make one yourself. My perception of the film business has been altered significantly since (in a good way). Everything is so much different now and it is hard to put into words, all I can say is I truly love my life.

> *"...it's the unplanned outcomes that make this all extraordinary."*

Q. What have been your biggest, unexpected rewards?

A: Some of the best footage in the film was totally unplanned. Life occurs the same way. Through this film, I learned it doesn't really matter how much you plan, the outcome is always different and it's the unplanned outcomes that make this all extraordinary. Isaac and I learned a new truth; that all there really is to do in life is show up and watch it unfold while

CHAD CAMERON

11

being in the middle of it. Everything in life occurs so perfectly when you live from true inspiration. What I've discovered is that when you act from inspiration, you don't have to force anything upon yourself that you are not inspired to do. The result is a higher level of freedom unlike anything I've ever felt before. I've never felt this free in my life before.

Q. Are there one or two things you can attribute your success to? Luck, timing, someone who helped you?

A. Just letting events unfold and not trying to force (or be attached) to any specific result. Lots of people told us that we needed a script for the movie, but we didn't have one. We tried to write the script and nothing ever felt right. The script ended up writing itself in the end. It all came together during the last month of production.

Q. What is the most important attribute you look for in an employee? Thoughts on the employee-ownership model?

A. I've learned through the years to listen to my gut on hiring. Both you and the person you hire should feel good about working together. If you have to force it, it never works out no matter how much you try. I suppose it's a bit of chemistry. I've always been a proponent of the employee-ownership model and we are getting involved in partnerships with others on other projects.

Q. Do you recommend any books or an MBA?

A. No on the MBA. I highly recommend Jed McKenna's books on spiritual enlightenment, they are some of the most amazing books I've ever read. *Busting Loose from the Money Game* by Robert Scheinfeld will cause you to question everything you thought you knew about life and money. *A Course in Miracles* by Helen Schucman and William Thetford is full of great concepts if you can get past the style of writing. Joe Vitale's *Zero Limits* and Dan Millman's *Way of the Peaceful Warrior*, which is probably one of the best introductions into the spiritual teachings of all the books I mentioned. What we tried to do with the *Leap!* movie was to condense all these teachings into a feature length documentary that we hope gives people a deeper understanding of multiple teachings.

Leap Ventures

Q. Slogan to live by or what it might say on your tombstone?

A. "Life is a game that is designed to be fun, if you're not having fun, do something else."

Q. Anything else that I didn't ask that would be wise advice to an aspiring entrepreneur?

A. The million dollar question is if you had a million dollars in the bank right now would you go to work tomorrow? If the answer is no then I would say you aren't doing the thing that is right for you. When people ask you about your plans and the future think about this: If I had asked you five or 10 years ago where you would be, would you have described the place you are now? I bet your answer would not only be no, but nowhere remotely close to what you had thought. So the next question I would ask you is, "Why are you spending so much time planning for the future?" If you could know the exact moment you were going to die, would you want to know? What if instead of waiting for everything to be perfect, you start living your dreams and aspirations now? I credit this final tidbit to the wisdom of a fortune cookie I once got. I did this with *Leap!* It could have easily been said that I did not have the money or time, but I made a movie that if people watch, will cause them to think for themselves.

CHAD CAMERON

About the movie, *LEAP!*

Leap! features interviews with over 20 people, including Dan Millman, Gary Renard, Fred Alan Wolf, James Twyman, Joe Vitale and many other philosophers, authors and spiritual leaders. The film uses ancient and modern philosophies to help people explore the idea of life as an illusion, and how to embrace that idea to transform your human experience. It is a complete paradigm shift in how you can live your life from a deep knowing of your true self. It offers a variety of different perspectives from spiritual visionaries and philosophers who have come to similar conclusions. Visit *www.leapmovie.com* to learn more or to purchase a copy of the DVD.

"The greatest danger for most of us is not that our aim is too high and we miss it, but that it is too low and we reach it."

- Michelangelo

4

"There is no Plan B."
Greg Clinard; Spinnato, Kropatsch, Clinard & Associates

◆

BACKGROUND

Greg Clinard is a partner in the firm Spinnato, Kropatsch, Clinard & Associates which was founded in 1978 by Mark Spinnato. They have two offices in Colorado and are headquartered in Westminster, Colorado. The firm currently employees 25 people in the financial services industry. He left behind a stable $60k/year salary job to embark on this current endeavor. In his prior life Greg was a self employed painting contractor.

INTERVIEW

Q: What was your initial startup cost?
A: I had a $15,000 buy in.

Q: How long until you had reached a positive cash flow?
A: Just 90 days!

Q: Did you use a business plan?
A: Yes, I did.

Q: Did you morph your original business plan to meet the demands of the market?
A: Yes, definitely, it's a living document. I spent the majority of time on the marketing aspect of the business plan. Sales of any type is a numbers game – activity generates leads, which creates prospect appointments, which results in sales. Hearing "no" a lot can have either a therapeutic or traumatic effect on someone. I accepted the "no's" since they meant a "yes" wasn't far behind.

Q: What was the genesis of the idea?

A: My best friend and college roommate, John, was in the financial planning business and one day showed me his paycheck and I was blown away by his earnings given the fact that we both began working at the same time. He was a recruiter for the financial services entity I now work with and the rest is history.

Q: What is the vision of the company and the community you serve?

A: The community we focus on are those interested in full financial planning and investment management. Our vision is to help our clients afford more time to do the things that are important to them, and to obtain security and peace of mind. Through a 'Q&A' with our clients, we take a look at the typical family as you would do to any small business, i.e. assets, liabilities, income, expenses, profit/loss, financial goals, etc. It's all about helping our clients reach the level of freedom they've worked so hard to obtain. The biggest misconception in our field is that it's only about the money, it's really not.

> *"It's all about helping our clients reach the level of freedom they've worked so hard to obtain."*

Q: What is the passion that it fills for you personally?
A: The drive to affect positive change in people's lives. To help them achieve their life goals is very fulfilling.

Q: Where do you see yourself and your company in 10 years?
A: To be in top 10 of financial planners in the area, with over 250 families as clients and managing over $100 million in assets.

Q: What have been your biggest challenges? What do you know now that you wish you had known sooner?
A: Dealing with self-destructive client behavior is not something I expected. Behavioral finance was a huge part of the career education, a part I wished was emphasized more in early training. Initially starting out, I thought that I would go right into financial planning, but quickly learned that market-

Spinnato, Kropatsch, Clinard & Associates

ing was going to take up the biggest part of my day.

Q: What aspects of ownership are the most rewarding and what has been your biggest reward?

A: Creating something from nothing. Within 10 years, I built a $1 million business that I can sell. The freedom of being self-employed allows me to be a better husband and a father.

Q: Are there one or two things you can attribute your success to? Luck, timing, someone who helped you?

A: My former fiancée's father was an entrepreneur and a positive influence on me. The one thing I always admired was the time he had to do all the things he enjoyed. My college roommate, John, also helped me get to this point in my life. Most of all though, was the idea that there is no Plan B. Having no Plan B in your mind is the only way you will ever truly succeed. It comes down to survival. I once read that some sailors who were stranded at sea in WWII survived because failure was not an option. If they had a family to return home to, their chances of survival were much greater. No Plan B is the idea of not having anything to fall back on. It's about going "all in" without knowing how you'll get it back, and not selling your time to an organization. It's about being compensated for your results without a salary cap.

> *"Having no Plan B in your mind is the only way you will ever truly succeed."*

GREG CLINARD

Q: How do you attract and retain the best employees? What is the most important attribute you look for? Any thoughts on the employee-ownership model?

A: In hiring people, we look for integrity, personality, and a burning entrepreneurial desire. When interviewing candidates, I try to uncover if they see the world of work from the perspective of entitlement or if they willing do to whatever it takes to add value. The ability to build equity in the company I work for is critical, do you want to rent or do you want to own? In our business we look for individuals with a thorough comprehension of financial planning and consultative sales. Fee-based practices, like ours in the financial services industry, earn money through GDC (gross dealer concessions) vs. commissions or transaction related activities. I firmly believe our company's success is the direct result of the employee ownership model, where all of our producers have equity in their part of the firm.

Q: Can you recommend any training or resources such as books, classes, or websites? Do you recommend an MBA?

A: No, I don't recommend an MBA. However, anything that helps you communicate better, sell better, and is motivating to you is a great tool. I got so much from Stephen Covey's *Seven Habits* books. I quote from them almost daily. Finance majors and/or MBA's don't usually make the best advisors because surprisingly, it's not about the math.

> *" I firmly believe our company's success is the direct result of the employee ownership model..."*

Q: Slogan to live by or what it might say on your tombstone?

A: "Work hard, play hard!" and "Live your life to the fullest and remember, there is no Plan B."

Spinnato, Kropatsch, Clinard & Associates

♦

"Make a difference. Get out of yourself and touch lives. When you focus on elevating others, you lift yourself. Life is a contact sport and it's all about collaboration."
Christine Comaford, Mighty Ventures LLC

BACKGROUND
Christine Comaford's life exemplifies the title 'serial entrepreneur'. She has a knack for being able to spot key trends and new technologies, and has built and sold five of her own businesses with an average 700% return on investment. She also has served as a board director or in-the-trenches advisor to thirty-six startups.

As a venture capitalist and angel investor, Christine has invested in over 200 startups. Christine's many reinventions have included being a Buddhist monk, a Microsoft engineer, a geisha trainee, and advisor to the White House. Christine was fortunate to enjoy an early retirement at age 40, but shortly thereafter she experienced the painful loss of her father to pancreatic cancer. As a way to cope with his death and further her own self-discovery, she began writing a memoir. The publisher she approached instead asked her to write a book about entrepreneurship, citing her unique knowledge and experience.

Her first book, *Rules for Renegades: How to Make More Money, Rock Your Career, and Revel in Your Individuality* came out in 2007 and soon become a #3 New York Times best seller, #2 Wall Street Journal bestseller, and #1 USA Today bestseller. For two days it was the bestselling book on all of Amazon.com.
In late 2006, Christine established Mighty Ventures, LLC where she and others consult with hundreds of startups, multi-national corporations, and the intrapreneurs within them to accelerate their business development and growth.

MIGHTY VENTURES, LLC

INTERVIEW

Q. Initial startup cost & source:
A: $300k (total funding to date).

Q. How long till positive cash flow?
A. We broke even in 2008.

Q. Did you use a business plan?
A. No, but we did write a business summary.

Q. The vision of the company & the community you serve?
A. We are business accelerators, serving both entrepreneurs of small startups and intrapreneurs in large corporations. We focus on business acceleration in three key areas: sales, marketing, and product path. Everything we do comes down to addressing the people, the money, and the model of the organizations we work with. The People: Who are the key people in the organization and do they have the right partners? Money: Does the business have the financing they need and are their sales able to sustain the business? Model: What's the market, how and when do they enter it to compete, are they growing their value and in turn market share? We do this for our clients via a year-long curriculum which includes group mentoring led by myself, one-on-one coaching, and retreats. We also do consulting projects and webinars.

> *"Everything we do comes down to addressing the people, the money, and the model of the organizations we work with."*

Q. The passion that it fills for you personally?
A. My passion is to make a difference. During a recent meditation, with amazing clarity, I had a vision of a circle; contribution was in the middle surrounded by the words 'reflection', 'connection', 'creativity', and 'community'. *Makeadifference. com* was the first domain I ever registered (I later sold it for $3000!).

Q. Where do you see yourself & your company in 10 years?

A. Because I build companies to sell them, without a doubt I can say 'not here'. I truly have no idea where I'll be. The only sure answer is 'anywhere' because I'm open to all possibilities.

Q. Biggest challenges? Looking back now, is there anything you wish you had done differently? What do you know now that you wish you'd known sooner?

A. The area I struggled with for much of my career was in working with others. For a long time, I truly believed that I had to do it all on my own. It wasn't until I turned 34 that I realized the difference the right team can make. I've had to learn to let go and allow others the space to contribute. You can have a much larger impact on the world if you can find others that click with you. I'm the first to admit that my style is unique and realize it's not for everyone. We only work with people who are ready to take committed immediate action, and this goes for my clients as well. I've learned that as a leader, my role is to be a conductor in a sense, to transfer energy to others. What I've learned in my 46 years is that life exists in the people you meet and the things you build together. You might build a friendship, a family, a product, a company, or an experience, but it's all about collaboration. I've discovered that it's when you put yourself out there that you experience the greatest personal growth. I can attest that a person can learn more in a deep one year relationship than in 7 years of celibacy.

Q. Biggest rewards? What aspects of ownership are the most rewarding? Any unexpected rewards?

A. Without a doubt, the biggest reward has been the success of our clients. It is not uncommon for them to double their revenue and triple their value in a year or less. We share their successes on our web site—it's super fulfilling. I love elevating others through fostering collaboration. I recently gave a speech to a large software company and they reported a 20% increase in sales for the quarter following that keynote address. I can't take full credit, but I am certain I made an impact. Something I get now is that I'm here to lift up others, and in that process I lift myself higher. It all comes back

Christine Comaford

to contribution. The key message I try to convey by example is that the more one contributes to others, the more they receive in return. The area I've found the greatest fulfillment lately is in getting behind others who become stars. I consider myself a 'star maker', and it's rewarding to see others in the limelight.

Q. Are there one or two qualities you can attribute your success to? Luck, timing, etc.

A. Tenacity. I owe my persistence to having to overcome adversity early in life. My dad wanted a son, he got a daughter. My dad told me at an early age things like, "You're not pretty." and "You're not very smart." At some point in my life, I realized I could make a choice; I could believe him and wallow in self pity and be a victim, or I could choose not to buy into it and define my own life. I know that everyone makes statements and decisions based on their own conditioning, based on the stories from their past they unknowingly cling to. My advice is: keep your ego in check. The world does not work for you, no matter who you are. It's something I first recognized with my dad who was also an entrepreneur and the more success you achieve, the harder it is to see this.

Q. What is the most important quality you look for in an employee? How do you attract and retain the best employees?

A. Initiative, responsibility and speed. I like those that create new things and challenge the status quo. If it's broken, fix it. In a startup, you can't wait to be told what to do. I need others around me who are out to make a difference, and have a sense of passion and purpose. Have a sense of ownership, take pride in your results, and don't pass off poor work or miss a deadline—or if you must, tell people in advance and explain why and when you will indeed deliver on your commitment. Know that what you are doing matters, and has an impact on everyone else. That's why I feel it's so important to all be working towards a vision bigger than ourselves. Especially when working with contrac-

> *"What I've learned in my 46 years is that life exists in the people you meet and the things you build together."*

MIGHTY VENTURES, LLC

tors, get behind a common goal. Then be sure to celebrate when you reach that goal. My best hires have always been based on personal recommendation and referrals. I love Craigslist but it's risky and time consuming. To retain my employees, I make sure they see their role in the bigger picture. Let yourself be real and human and flawed with them; give them lots of appreciation.

> *"Something I get now is that I'm here to lift up others, and in that process I lift myself higher. It all comes back to contribution."*

Q. Recommended training & resources?

A. After a lifetime of taking personal development courses, the very best one, hands down, is The Hoffman Institute. It is seven days of intense training where you uncover the patterns in your life and where you got them. Being aware of them allows you to let them go or at least reduce their impact. Of course, Rules for Renegades was a best seller for a reason. It's practical, real world knowledge that's also fun to read.

Q. How do you define success and fulfillment?

A. Joy and peace. If I died tomorrow I'd say I rocked it. At some point I finally realized that I am enough, I do enough and I have enough. I've gained the perspective from my hospice work that we don't have long and there's no point in putting things off. We die a little each time we compromise ourselves and put off those things we know in our heart we must do. I believe that fulfillment exists in moments, but it's not sustainable because it's always moving forward. You feel fulfilled, then some time passes and you stretch and you grow and you have new experiences. You say to yourself, now I want the next level. I didn't know the penthouse existed when I was in the basement. I thought the basement was all there was. I find that as I get more and more in touch with who I am, why I'm here, and what my gifts are, I can love so much more deeply than I ever thought was possible. I think a lot of people get in trouble because they think that life should be like Club Med and they think "Hey, where's the good looking

CHRISTINE COMAFORD

person with the cocktails?". But life isn't Club Med. Life is this amazing university with a spectacular course catalog and brilliant instructors and many of the courses are mandatory—like compassion, love, accountability, communication—we just don't know this when we're young!

Q. How do you deal with adversity today?

A. Whenever I come across something that I get upset by I ask two questions. 1) How important is this in the grand scheme of things? 2) What's the lesson in this? I believe there's a great lesson in everything, and in knowing that part of me needs to grow because I brought this situation into my life. My dad said cancer was the best thing that ever happened to him, after my mom. He said Nancy was first but that cancer was second because it helped him see how valuable his life was. It enabled him to turn his life around in his last four months. So, I totally believe in crash course life lessons. My dad got to have that peace and he got to really feel love before he died. He graduated. Who cares if you cram? If you pass the exam it doesn't matter.

> *"I owe my persistence to having to overcome adversity early in life."*

Q. Slogan to live by or what it might say on your tombstone?

A. "Make a difference. Get out of yourself and touch lives. When you focus on elevating others, you lift yourself. Life is a contact sport and it's all about collaboration."

Q. Is there anything else you want to share?

A. As the founder, it's hard but important to not get attached to your own company. I call it 'founderitis' when people botch financing and acquisitions because they feel their company is more valuable than it is. Then, of course, no one else comes along later and the company goes under. Instead, think of your company as a living, breathing organism and it's your responsibility simply to be the caretaker and the shepherd for a period of time. Sometimes it's for a lifetime but you have to pay attention and ask, "What's the best thing for this

MIGHTY VENTURES, LLC

living, breathing company?" For it to be fully evolved and a part of something bigger, you have to just get out of the way. Be careful that your company doesn't simply become an extension of your ego.

It's like children. When people treat a child as an extension of their ego it's not good for the kid and it's not good for the parent. You never made it in soccer and you're trying to make your kid a soccer star and that doesn't resonate with the kid , so let it go. Let the kid be who they are. It's important to realize that it's similar with companies. If you bring other people into the company, which you will, you need to let them shape the culture. It's not about you. As entrepreneurs, we often to have a lot of arrogance and ego because we had to survive those early adversities, if not, we wouldn't have the mindset of an entrepreneur.

Entrepreneurs have a healthy dissatisfaction. I think if you're totally happy with the way everything is going and you don't really feel any need to make a big contribution or whatever, then keep doing what you're doing. I think that a lot of people just have dissatisfaction and don't do anything about it. Then there's a healthy dissatisfaction that motivates you to move forward, to stretch and to grow.

I really want people to know that entrepreneurs aren't special. So often people say, "Well, I couldn't do that because x, y, z. I don't have the education. I don't have the pedigree. I don't have this or that. I'm not that smart." It's about finding what you really care about. Find what you love and that which you're good at. The point at which these intersect with what the market needs is a sustainable business. If your business will help people make money, save money, or remove pain, you're golden.

> *"At some point I finally realized that I am enough, I do enough and I have enough."*

Find a mentor. Find someone who's been there when the grenades were flying or you will be like so many entrepreneurs who come to Mighty Ventures after burning through all their cash. You don't have to go through all that pain and suffering, all those mistakes, if you just find good mentors. And be sure it's someone you are in contact with often.

Jump on my *Results Now* call (www.resultsnowcall.com), it's free and it will help you figure out how to rock your marketing (make a thousand new leads per month), sales (disqualify and close faster) and team (help them become self-managed and highly effective). We also do free calls every month at AskChristineNow.com . People submit their business questions and I answer as many as I can.

MIGHTY VENTURES, LLC

6

"Try as much as you can, no matter how much you fail."
John Comeau, Horsetooth Hot Sauce

◆

BACKGROUND

John Comeau and his wife, Allie, founded Horsetooth Hot Sauce, a retail and wholesale food company, in 2008 in Fort Collins, Colorado. When he was laid off in early 2008, and couldn't find work, the necessity of making a living became the genesis for his company. John had no prior food company experience, but making hot sauce was something he had always enjoyed as a hobby. His wife encouraged him to start the business, since she had already been self employed for many years. The fact that she is in marketing and copywriting has helped them significantly. John likes the appeal of producing a locally made product. He has two employees, and in the future hopes to expand their product line beyond hot sauce to build a "Horsetooth Foods" brand.

JOHN COMEAU

INTERVIEW

Q: What was your initial startup cost and source?
A: $4k, credit cards

Q: How long until there was a positive cash flow?
A: We have not hit a positive cash flow just yet.

Q: Did you use a business plan? If so, have you had to modify your original business plan to meet the demands of the market?
A: Yes. I have spent time mainly on revising the financial aspects of the business plan.

Q: What is the vision of the company and the community you serve?
A: I enjoyed making hot sauce as a hobby. I also have always

seen the appeal of buying locally made products. Now I'm getting the opportunity to work with many other local businesses, restaurants and retail shops, and am proud to participate in the "local" economy.

> *"I learned a lot through tutorials on YouTube, especially when it came to label and business card design..."*

Q: What is the passion that your business fills for you personally?

A: I love people, and especially the people like me, who also love hot sauce! It is great being around people who share your passion for something. The freedom of being my own boss has been great.

Q: What was the genesis of the idea?

A: It was really the necessity of having to make a living when I couldn't find employment.

Q: Where do you see yourself and your company in 10 years?

A: We'd like to expand our product line beyond hot sauce, and build a "Horsetooth Foods" brand.

Q: What were your biggest challenges?

A: The health department, and all the licensing required to sell a food product. Everything from the font size on the labels to having to convince the FDA that it was not an "acid" food.

Q: What aspects of ownership are the most rewarding?

A: I'd have to say it has been the freedom, but also the joy of selling a product I really believe in.

Q: Are there one or two things you can attribute your success to?

A: My wife has been the biggest supporter, which helped me push on.

Q: What is the most important attribute you look for in an employee?

A: I look for passion, pride in the product, and knowledge.

HORSETOOTH HOT SAUCE

Q: Any recommended books or other resources? Do you recommend an MBA?

A: No on the MBA. Michael Gerber's *E-Myth* was a valuable book. I learned a lot through tutorials on YouTube, especially when it came to label and business card design (Adobe Illustrator tutorials).

Q: Slogan to live by or what it might say on your tombstone?

A: "Try as much as you can, no matter how much you fail."

JOHN COMEAU

"Our calling is the point at which our deepest gladness meets the world's deepest need."

- Frederick Buechner

7

"The world is run by those who show up."
John Fischer, Sticker Giant

◆

BACKGROUND

John Fischer started StickerGiant, *www.stickergiant.com*, in 2000. Today he has eight full time employees and five part-time in Hygiene, Colorado. What began for John as a curiosity, at a time when he was home sick with the flu, *WhatPresident.com*, quickly became an overnight national sensation during the five week period when the USA didn't know who its president was, Gore or Bush! The slogan, "He is not my president," died as quickly as it grew, but along the way, sold thousands of stickers, mugs, and T-shirts. From that experience, the vision for Sticker-Giant began to grow in John's mind. He partnered with a young designer, Mike Brooks, on building a brand that was hip, and fed the demand for stickers that reflected all things in our pop culture. Do a Google search for the word "stickers," and *sticker-giant.com* is number one. StickerGiant's stickers are all over the world and beyond. They even have StickerGiant stickers in the Space Shuttle!

INTERVIEW

Q: What was your initial startup cost and source?
A: $80,000 from personal savings and credit cards.

Q: How long until there was a positive cash flow?
A: Twelve months. I started making a profit just about the time I ran out of money and credit.

Q: Did you use a business plan?
A: Yes, and I recommend it for the sole purpose of having a communication tool others can give you feedback on. It's a good reality check.

Q: What was the genesis of the idea?

A: I was an avid collector of stickers as a kid, back to the days of the "Garbage Pail Kids" stickers. My entire career always centered around printing. Stickers are one of the earliest forms of social media. Stickers provide a way for others to personally endorse something. It gives people a voluntary way to show their support and pride for something. What's more effective, a sticker on a car or a billboard? I would argue the former, and it's one of the lowest cost forms of advertising. Of all the Obama stickers you see today, nobody is paying them to put them up, but the impact of them has no doubt contributed to who our next president will be. I'm a firm believer that everyone should have the right to voice their opinion, and stickers provide an effective way to do so.

Q: What is the vision of the company and the community you serve? What came first, the problem or the solution?

A: Stickers have been around since the 1920's, in the form of tin signs on the back of Model T's. There was no single source out there, and the internet provided a vehicle to sell stickers in a way they had never been sold before. Simply stated; we sell stickers, and we create custom stickers. On the retail side, pre-designed, we have over 20,000 different designs, ranging from political to music groups to wall stickers; think children's rooms, and scrapbooking. We have an online tool to upload your own custom designs. Two years ago we started offering custom print services. That portion of our business is now more than twice the size of our retail pre-made stickers. We focus on the design, sales, and marketing aspects of the business.

Q: Where do you see yourself and your company in 10 years?

A: *Stickergiant.com* is larger but still somewhere in Boulder County. Essentially, doing what I am now, and I have no intention of selling the business. I want to make it easier for people to share their passions, and get their ideas out to the world.

Q: Looking back now, is there anything you wish you had done differently?

STICKER GIANT

A: I have no regrets. I suppose I could look back, and say I wish I would have taken more risk and hired more people sooner, but I have no idea on whether or not that would have made a difference, good or bad. I'm not a risk taker, and perhaps that has allowed me to weather some of the down economic cycles.

Q: What aspects of ownership are the most rewarding?

A: The biggest reward is getting to work with people I like. Coming into work every day and working with such a fun and cool group is the best reward. I also love our customers! Through this company, I've met some of the neatest people that I never would have otherwise met. In general, the excitement of being an entrepreneur, and having full creativity and freedom to do things the way I want.

Q: Are there one or two things you can attribute your success to? Was it luck, timing, someone who helped you?

A: I was lucky in that I had good parents, and grew up in a supportive family in the USA. Beyond that, I believe you must create your own luck. Early in my career, I am thankful that the jobs I held were commission-based. It caused an appreciation for how businesses make money on a day to-day basis. I'd suggest you work for a smaller company right out of college to get that kind of experience firsthand. Too many college kids today go right into large corporations, only to be so far removed that they never learn the basics of how a company makes money, or for that matter, how to manage their own finances. I come from a family of entrepreneurs that was always there to support me, and offer valuable advice.

> *"I suppose I could look back, and say I wish I would have taken more risk and hired more people sooner, but I have no idea on whether or not that would have made a difference, good or bad."*

Q: What is the most important attribute you look for in an employee? What are your thoughts on the employee-ownership model?

JOHN FISCHER

A: I began by hiring part-time stay-at-home moms to help pack and ship the stickers I sold online. While we don't have an employee ownership stake today, our business model doesn't yet support it, I am an advocate for it. Right now we are focused on near term profitability to sustain our growth.

Q: Any recommended training and resources? Books, classes, websites? Do you recommend an MBA?

A: No on the MBA. Learning by doing is far more valuable. The sooner you start failing, the sooner you'll learn the truth of what it takes to be successful. I believe in hiring MBA's because you need some of that knowledge to keep your business healthy. Books by Malcom Gladwell such as *The Tipping Point* and *Outliers*. Also *The Long Tail* by Chris Anderson and Noah Goldstein's, *Yes! 50 Scientifically Proven Ways to be Persuasive*. Right now I'm reading, *Call to Action* by Bryan Eisenberg, Jeffrey Eisenberg, and Lisa T. Davis. I'm also a fan of Guy Kawasaki's books. Most importantly, surround yourself with your peer group; this has been a key to my success. I belong to several entrepreneur groups that meet on a regular basis. It's not something I naturally have a tendency to do, as I tend to be a workaholic, but have realized the importance of getting out, and interacting with others. Also, getting heavily involved in social media has been huge for us.

> *"Most importantly, surround yourself with your peer group; this has been a key to my success."*

Q: Slogan to live by or what it might say on your tombstone?
A: "The world is run by those who show up."

Q: Is there anything else you'd like to add?
A: One of the best ways to tap into the power of viral marketing is to offer your sticker to anyone who sends you a SASE, a self-addressed stamped envelope. It costs you nothing but the time to put a sticker in the SASE, but in doing so, you enable the word of mouth about you to spread. Think about it, someone sees a sticker on your notebook, and they ask you about it. You've now created a conversation, and begun to spread the word virally.

STICKER GIANT

8

"Helping business owners reach greater personal and business success."
Allen Fishman, The Alternative Board®

◆

BACKGROUND

Allen Fishman established The Alternative Board (TAB®) in 1990. TAB provides peer board and coaching services for business owners and CEOs in over 400 cities around the world. Today TAB has over 150 franchisees and 35 full-time employees. Allen's first company, Infinite Horizons Training Systems, is a business education system. His second venture; *Sun Development Company* built, and currently manages, shopping centers and office buildings. He still holds controlling interest in these companies. In 1980, Allen became a part owner, President & COO in Tipton Centers Inc. (TCI), a consumer electronics retailer, which Allen took public in 1986 before it was acquired by Dixon in 1987. Following the sale of TCI, at the age of 45, Fishman retired to Aspen, Colorado area where he wrote the nationally syndicated advice column, *Business Insights*. While doing interviews for the column, he identified the key factors common to those entrepreneurs who had achieved success that led him to author two books: *7 Secrets of Great Entrepreneurial Masters: The GEM Power™ Formula for Lifelong Success* and *9 Elements of Family Business Success*. In addition to being featured in The Wall Street Journal, USA Today, Fortune Small Business, Business Week, The Los Angeles Times, and the Chicago Tribune, Allen hosted the radio show *Formula for Success* on a CBS, and is a frequent guest on CNBC, Bloomberg, and CNNfn.

INTERVIEW

Q: What was your initial startup cost?
A: A mid six figure investment from my own resources.

Q: How long till positive cash flow should a start up business owner expect?

A: I did not need a salary. I made a deep commitment of my time to bringing business owners a new way of strategic thinking about running their businesses and their lives. My answer would depend on the type of business; you can open a hot dog stand and be profitable in the first month, or you can create a business that consumes capital for years before achieving positive returns. Companies that provide early profitability on low capital are less likely to achieve seven figure profits. One mistake that entrepreneurs frequently make is forgetting to allow for their personal needs. This creates stresses in the family and can prevent them from being able to stay in the game long enough to make the business a success. It is important for the owner to know the cost to sustain an adequate lifestyle, and plan for the necessary cash flow.

Q: Did you use a business plan?

A: Yes, I'm a strong believer in processes and taking the time to do analysis so that you make your move strategically. One of the big mistakes with business owners is that they go right to an action plan, rather than taking the time first to define their personal vision for success. This vision is unique to every individual. After the personal vision is determined the entrepreneur needs a company vision that supports the personal goals. And after that, you need to list the critical success factors for the business, and identify the one critical factor that will be the primary focus of your attention. This analysis should be completed before a business plan can be drawn up. Even then the entrepreneur should not write an action plan. You have to start with a clear, measurable, time related goal, write up the strategies to achieve the goal, and then write your action plan.

> *"One mistake that entrepreneurs frequently make is forgetting to allow for their personal needs."*

Implementing the action plan is another process that needs to be controlled. Owners can get entangled in putting out day-to-day fires, and fail to deal with real roadblocks. One common difficulty is establishing alignment among the staff. This entails assessment of behaviors to nurture cooperation instead of competition and conflict. We have identified six primary sources of roadblocks that should be avoided if a great action plan is to deliver great success.

Q: So, the planning process is like a living document?

A: There's an expression "It's evergreen". No business plan should be stagnant. The owner should be constantly reviewing the plan based on new facts. A year ago your plan may not have anticipated the current recession. Many companies that thought "What worked before will work again" are in trouble. The companies that we see doing well have changed course by identifying new critical factors and modifying their plan based on today's circumstances.

Q: The genesis of the idea for TAB?

A: It took place at a party. A few business owners were talking about the fact that they had needs that they could not discuss with employees or family members. They had no place to get real advice, no support group. That night it hit me that they had been quite comfortable talking about this situation among themselves. The next day we skied together and I asked them, "What if I could provide you with a professional who would facilitate a group meeting once a month and coach you during the month?" They liked the idea and the company was launched.

Q: What came first, the problem or the solution?

A: The problem. Once I had identified the need, the solution was something that I became passionate about. I was already writing business columns and doing talks that discussed these types of things. So, the key was, could I take some of methodologies that I talked about, or that I wrote about, and train others to replicate the same process? From that we created a written process that, with minor modifications, works for almost any privately held company. The process is a formalized version of what I used at TCI. Our coaching process is called Strategic Business Leadership, and it is now a web-based service.

Q: What is the passion that it fulfills for you personally?

A: I enjoy seeing how our process impacts not only the business's success, but enables business owners to recognize that business success means nothing if it doesn't lead to their personal vision of success. An extreme example was a TAB board member that I met at an airport who told me that I had saved his life. This was nothing that I had done personally. He had a daughter who had serious problems. Her difficulties distracted him so much that they were destroying his business and his marriage. He brought the matter to his TAB board and found that others had survived similar experiences. The board's support enabled him to keep it together and deal with the problems, what he called a life-saving service.

Today, my son-in-law does runs the business as President and CEO. This allows me to focus on the parts of the company operations that part of it that I enjoy, which is public speaking on current business topics, program development, and the continuing management of the original founder's board, which still has several of the original members from 1990. We are all a little older now but still practicing the core methodology.

Q: Where do you see yourself & your company in 10 years?

A: The Alternative Board is expanding into more countries and I hope to see it influence many more lives. From the start I hired highly talented staff to run the day-to-day operations. TAB members are very bright successful people and you have to have outstanding people to support them. My expectation is that I will be strategically involved with the company to create the methodologies and the programs, not to get involved in managing any of the people. Right now I am refining and formalizing a program I developed for Infinite Horizons Training Systems, that deals with the 14 most common mistakes in managing sales and I am delighted to know that it has been well received.

> *"Once I had identified the need, the solution was something that I became passionate about."*

THE ALTERNATIVE BOARD®

Q: What were your biggest challenges? Looking back now, is there anything you wish you had done differently?

A: When I formed The Alternative Board I required little structure from the people who are facilitating and coaching. After a period of time I realized that that wasn't good enough and we needed a uniform offering providing the same value to all members wherever they are located. For example, it is very important that somebody coaching in Oakland, California coaches with the same materials, the same SBL process and the same soft skills as somebody coaching in London. It took awhile to correct that mistake. That's the competitive edge of our TAB facilitator coaches.

Q: What aspects of ownership are the most rewarding? Any unexpected rewards?

A: Having the opportunity to travel to many cities as an invited speaker. It is most rewarding when people in the audience come up to tell me what TAB and Strategic Business Leadership has done for their lives. Also, when I started TAB I didn't have a son-in-law so I never anticipated that my son-in-law would become CEO of the company.

Q: Are there one or two things you can attribute your success to, luck, timing, or someone who helped you?

A: I was fortunate to have natural ability and to be born into a family where my father and my uncle were in business together. As a teenager I worked in the business and they talked business with me at the dinner table. I studied for degrees in finance and accounting and I got my law degree, but I had the added knowledge of how business works.

Q: How do you attract and retain the best employees? What Is the most important attribute you look for?

A: First, I look for people whose ability matches the job being filled. Some jobs require a certain God given ability, but a genius would be bored with the same task. So we do general intelligence tests as a first step to match the skill levels.

Next, I look for passion and I ask them to talk about that passion to find out if they are actually knowledgeable about

ALLEN FISHMAN

the subject they say they are interested in. I use the experience that I have gained from interacting with entrepreneurs running businesses of every description, to determine if they are genuine or just telling me what they think I want to hear.

Q: Do you recommend an MBA for an entrepreneur?

A: No. At the same time I will tell you that one of my members on the founder's board just got his MBA and feels that getting an MBA has been very good for him. He is a second generation in the business, and for a lot of reasons he felt he had not been exposed to things outside his business and the MBA rounded off his knowledge base. But generally speaking I'd say no because most MBA's are geared to teaching how to work for someone else.

I talked to one TAB board member with an MBA program who told me he felt that his MBA had been a waste because the people teaching him were not entrepreneurs. They taught nuts and bolts, but they didn't really understand the entrepreneurial mindset. That's one of the keys to success as an entrepreneur. It's also one of the reasons why many businesses that are successful while they are being driven by an entrepreneur, but fail when they are acquired by a big company and run by professional managers. It's a different mindset.

Q: Do you have any recommended training or resources for entrepreneurs?

A: When you talk about books clearly I'd like them to read my books, I strongly recommend my book, 7 Secrets of Great Entrepreneurial Masters: The GEM Power™ Formula for Lifelong Success which is heavily directed towards what somebody should be thinking about when they are starting a business. If the business is a family business, I recommend my book, 9 Elements of Family Business Relationships.

I now think that some of the best information is to be found on the Web where you can target your search and the diversity of available information is mind boggling. Reading a book requires attention to sections that are not the target of your search.

Q: Slogan to live by or what it might say on your tombstone?
A: It wouldn't have anything to do with business. It would be that "Family is everything." That doesn't mean that it's right for others. It's that it's right for me.

Q: Do you have a mastermind group?
A: I facilitate the founder's TAB peer board group. A peer board shares the entrepreneurial advice that can only come from someone who is outside of the business you know. It provides those "out of box" ideas because you're not locked into the same thinking as someone in any particular business field. When I ran the Tipton Centers there were eighteen companies across the country that met several times a year to share ideas. It was a great benefit but there were a few problems, nobody facilitated the meetings and there was no coaching. But the biggest problem was that we were all from the same industry. In TAB peer boards, where the members have to be from different kinds of companies, the best ideas frequently come from somebody who knows nothing about your industry.

Q: Anything else?
A: For those who own a company, I recommend that they get together with other business owners. Obviously I would steer them to join a TAB board, but there are other peer board organizations and, by and large, they do a good job. I believe that peer board participation is essential to maximize the probability of success. For those considering a new business, I have already talked about defining the vision and the strategy before the action plan. I would recommend consideration of franchises that are associated with some personal passion. If your passion is automobiles, find a business in that field. The statistics show that the probability of success is much greater if the business matches the individual's personal strengths.

"Every new day begins with possibilities. It's up to us to fill it with the things that move us towards progress and peace."

- Ronald Reagan

9

"All information ever created is still in existence."
Thomas Frey, The DaVinci Institute

◆

BACKGROUND

Thomas Frey began The DaVinci Institute in 1997, a think tank now based in Louisville, Colorado. The DaVinci Institute is a futurist non-profit organization which produces many distinctive events each month designed to change people's lives. The events include boot camps and crash courses for business leaders and entrepreneurs, as well as networking events. Tom worked at IBM full-time, but he felt something inside him wanting more out of life. So he put on his entrepreneurial hat in his personal time away from IBM, and has since started 17 businesses!

INTERVIEW

Q: What was your initial startup cost and source?

A: Nothing. I exited my property management company and made a transition. I had a small office space and furniture that I carried over to my new venture. I tried to be as creative as possible to keep our costs down.

Q: How long until you reached a positive cash flow?

A: One year. I created a traveling seminar, *Inventions of Impact*, which helped move the business into new territory. I did a couple tours around the country where I was a one-man road show and lived life as a traveling speaker and trainer for a while.

Q: What was the genesis of the idea?

A: Well, when I began The DaVinci Institute, I focused on doing some consulting work to make ends meet. In 2002, we began producing events. The 2003 *Future of Money Summit* was our first big event and it was a major milestone because many people started paying attention to us. We bootstrapped the

THOMAS FREY

entire thing.

Q: Did you use a business plan?

A: No, not a formal one. Startup businesses often wrestle with writing a business plan, but in the end, they're pretty meaningless. A good startup entrepreneur realizes that business is always changing, never static. They have to react instantly to new information and compensate for changing market conditions. Business plans are built around a snapshot in time, often false assumptions, miracles that may never happen.

Q: What is the vision of your organization?

A: To help people unlock their future one idea, one invention, one business at a time. Presently, we focus on just two areas of assistance for entrepreneurs - holding networking events and providing education. We run two networking events a month, *Night with a Futurist* and *Startup Junkie Underground*. They are designed to bring people together who are synergistically linked to the startup world. I often tell people to surround themselves with people who look like what they want to become. For education, we hold boot camps once a month. Different strategies, market niches, and technologies are explored. The boot camps work very well because the teachers are real world experts in their field, talking about real-world lessons and real-world failures.

Q: What is the passion this field that touches you personally?

A: Being around startup entrepreneurs is very inspirational. These are the risk-takers, creating the disruptive technologies, learning from their mistakes, building durable lifestyles where every failure is just another opportunity to move forward. I love being around these people. Funny thing is, I was a loner when I first started out.

> *"A good startup entrepreneur realizes that business is always changing, never static. "*

Q: Where do see yourself and your company in 10 years?

A: We are working to develop the world's first museum of future inventions. It is a huge undertaking, but we have created what appears to be a reasonable path for getting there.

DaVinci Institute

I know this is a project that will take years to complete and I haven't deluded myself into thinking it will be easy.

Q: What were your biggest challenges?

A: When I first started, I had to shift my thinking from finding my next boss to finding my next client. I've reached a point where I am now part of the hard core unemployable. I will never be able to go back to working a 9-5 job for someone else. The wiring in my head has changed, hopefully for the better.

> *"Get rid of your safety nets. Every day is an adventure."*

Q: What do you know now that you wish you had known sooner? On a similar note, is there anything you wish you had done differently?

A: If you don't pay attention to the money, everything starts to fall apart. Anyone who survives in the startup world has come to that conclusion sooner or later. As a startup entrepreneur, you will often get asked the question, "Why don't you just get a regular job?" This question will come up often while you are struggling through the early stages to takeoff. You will need to be prepared for this question, create an answer first for yourself, and turn it into a compelling reason that others can grasp.

Q: What aspects of ownership are the most rewarding?

A: When you are an entrepreneur the highs are higher and the lows are lower. Get rid of your safety nets. Every day is an adventure. Live it like you mean it.

Q: What do you consider to be your greatest accomplishments?

A: Making a transition from the corporate world to being an entrepreneur is a major accomplishment. While I received over 270 awards while I was at IBM, more than any other engineer, I rate my accomplishments today in the number of lives that I have the opportunity to touch. I speak to audiences totaling 10,000 people a year. The papers and articles I write reach far more than that.

THOMAS FREY

Q: Are there one or two things you can attribute your success to?

A: Good genetics. My dad was a farmer, so I was the child of an entrepreneur. **Persistence.** No one can succeed in this world without extreme persistence and that's been one of my long suits. **Loyalty.** I believe that in order for anyone to truly succeed, you have to have an unusual amount of loyalty to what you are doing. You have to take ownership of it on so many different levels. **Confidence.** Ask yourself "Have I earned the right to be here?" You will always have doubt, and that's okay. You need to get comfortable with being uncomfortable.

Q: How do you attract and retain the best employees?

A: Most of our employees are part-time people working under contract. However, the projects we are working on tend to attract inspired people. In the future I see the idea of long-term employment falling by the wayside. Business units are getting smaller, to the point where most businesses in the future will be one-person operations, something I've dubbed the 'Empire of One' business model. This is where everyone is a free agent doing project-based work. Nearly all work is outsourced, requiring no HR department. The people work very hard, but they work when they want to. It's a very appealing business model.

Q: Are there any books, classes or training you recommend?

A: Of course. For starters I would suggest anyone looking to get more out of their life, to first check out the DaVinci Institute, *www.davinciinstitute.com*. In fact, I'd also recommend they visit "Ten Rules for Bootstrapping Your Business" by searching our website [see also *Appendix B*]. Also, I suggest they read as many futurist and business minded books as they can, such as *Revolutionary Wealth* by Alvin Toffler and *The Long Tail* by Chris Anderson. One last thing I'll mention is your readers should keep abreast of the world by reading blogs like the *Impact Lab* (www.impactlab.com); *Slashdot* (www.slashdot.org), and

> *"I believe that in order for anyone to truly suceed, you have to have an unusual amount of loyalty to what you are doing."*

eMarketer (www.eMarketer.com). Also, listen to tech and business podcasts like *TWIT* and *Dignation*. You can never know too much.

Q: Would you recommend an MBA?

A: No. Not for becoming an entrepreneur. MBAs work well in the corporate world but have little relevance to startups. Colleges can teach you many things, but they can't teach you the emotional side of business. They can't teach you what it feels like to have your world collapse around you, to get handed a lawsuit, or watch your own bank account go to zero. These things are very emotional and you just need to experience them. They are all gut checks to see if you are cut out for what you want to do.

> *"Your business is never about there, here, and now. It is always about the future."*

Q: Slogan to live by or what it might say on your tombstone?

A: "Adversity causes some people to break, and others to break records." I'm not a big fan in thinking in terms of tombstone legacies. They're rather trite and speak only for the moment. I tend to focus most of my thinking around ideas of the future. "All information ever created is still in existence." Is it possible for people in the future to view us today? "Who's the most famous person of all time?" In asking this question, my assumption is that the most famous person of all times hasn't been born yet. So what is it that this future person will have accomplished? This is the kind of thinking that keeps me energized and engaged.

Q: Anything else you may like to add?

A: When starting a business, keep you peripheral vision intact as you look across the opportunity landscape. Your business is never about there here and now. It is always about the future.

THOMAS FREY

"It's easy to choose success over failure, riches over poverty, any dream over the alternative. What's hard to do is to re-choose the same goal, dream, and level of success every day, every single hour, until it becomes reality. While it's easy to choose success and riches, it's not easy to carry through with your thoughts every single hour of every day. The difference maker is choosing to be one of the most successful people you know, every hour of every day for the rest of your life!"

- Brad Sugars

10

"Do good and be happy."
Dan Ganousis, AccelChip

◆

BACKGROUND
Dan joined AccelChip in 2001. Based in San Jose, AccelChip was best known in the Electronic Design Automation (EDA) industry for creating the first synthesis tool of the MATLAB® programming language for IC design. AccelChip employed 21 people before being sold to Xilinx in 2006. Dan has been instrumental in 13 other startups and offers himself as a CEO for hire, offering sweat equity for the right opportunity.

INTERVIEW
Q: What was your initial startup cost and source?
A: $1.1 million from angel investors, $7.1 million in series B and C rounds from venture capitalist's and strategic partners.

Q: How long until you had reached a positive cash flow?
A: 28 months.

Q: Did you use a business plan?
A: Yes.

Q: Have you had to morph your original business plan to meet the demands of the market?
A: The business plan changed to match our knowledge of the market, and to keep pace with our competitors. We updated the business plan quarterly, mostly around sales strategies (i.e. recreating the value proposition, compressing the sales cycle, and seek new ways to generating revenue).

Q: What was the genesis of the idea?
A: The technology was developed at Northwestern University

DAN GANOUSIS

ACCELCHIP

> *"The most important thing I can share in becoming an effective leader is that you have to have nerves of steel."*

and was licensed to AccelChip through the Northwestern Technology Transfer Office. In the end, the university benefited financially from the sale of AccelChip and today AccelChip serves as a showcase 'success story' that they strive for in other technology transfers.

Q: What is the vision of the company and the community you serve? Did the problem or need come first?

A: To speed the development of research to production is the ultimate goal of EDA (Electronic Design Automation). It's all about bridging technology to an end product. AccelChip was established to monetize intellectual property that the university owned. A problem definitely existed – what was needed was advanced research which ultimately came from the university.

Q: What is the passion that it fills for you personally?

A: Earning a good living (the financial gains), independence and freedom, and ultimately the reward that comes from working hard and being successful.

Q: Where do you see yourself and your company in 10 years?

A: Living in both the US and Costa Rica. In Costa Rica I'll spend my days writing. I've always been a writer on the side, and am currently penning *A Grumpy Old Guy's Guide to Startup Marketing*. When in Colorado, I'd like to continue officiating high school football and umpiring college baseball.

Q: Is there anything you have learned that could have helped you in the beginning?

A: Some valuable lessons I've learned along the way: Don't hire sales and marketing people before the product is truly ready; big money makes good people do bad things (greed); never keep the existing management of a company you take over (or are asked to run) because "a fish rots from the head first"; the geography you select to start your business will limit your access to investment capital.

Q: What aspects of ownership are the most rewarding?

A: Having the financial means to truly enjoy life and live to the fullest. At one time, being able to take an entire year off. The big payoff in the end is the moment you start generating revenue, you get on the success slope and the validation that the idea will fly is very rewarding.

Q: Are there one or two things you can attribute your success to? Luck, timing, someone who helped you?

A: Networking has been huge. I am grateful to have access to so many powerful people. The most important thing I can share in becoming an effective leader is that you have to have nerves of steel. In the face of those you lead, no matter what is going on with the company, you have to maintain a strong image. There are times it will get really tough, but above all,

> *"You will make many mistakes along the way, learn from them."*

strive to maintain your composure. Don't let your employees sense any weakness or you limit what they can achieve. The times when the company is at it's lowest is when you will need to be most creative and maintain your cool. Any doubt needs to be left at the door of your office – never, ever let your fears be known.

Q: How do you attract and retain the best employees? What is the most important attribute you look for? Thoughts on the employee-ownership model?

A: I look to hire people who aspire to be somewhere in their career where they're not currently, but have a strong desire to get there. I'm driven (as a coach) to help people get to the next level. Employee ownership is essential, I wouldn't work for a company unless it exists. The ideal model is 10-15% of the equity of a company goes to senior management; 5% to the CEO, 2% to the CTO, and the rest distributed to the other VPs. Having a financial event exist at some point in time is key; ownership has a bigger impact to motivate when everyone is striving for a specific result.

Q: Can you recommend any training or resources such as books,

DAN GANOUSIS

classes, or websites? Do you recommend an MBA?

A: I don't feel an MBA is important. You should put your time into building relationships. Find people who are 10-15 years older than you and network with them, learn from them and see them as your mentors. You will make many mistakes along the way, learn from them. What you learn in a classroom likely won't help in a startup. Never stop learning from people and your experiences.

Q: Slogan to live by or what it might say on your tombstone?
A: "Do good and be happy" – only you can choose this.

AccelChip

"It isn't what you know, but what you are determined to do that makes the difference. Knowing actually gets in the way."
Michael Gerber, E-Myth Worldwide®

◆

BACKGROUND

Michael Gerber is best known for his worldwide bestseller, *The E-Myth Revisited*, where he dispels the myths surrounding starting your own business and shows how commonplace assumptions can get in the way of running a business. He walks the reader through the steps in the life of a business from infancy, through adolescent growing pains, to the mature entrepreneurial perspective. He shows how applying the lessons of franchising can help any business. Michael stresses the distinction between working **on** your business, compared to working **in** your business. His company, E-Myth Worldwide, was founded in 1977 and is based in Santa Rosa, CA. With over 70 full-time employees and licensees around the world, E-Myth Worldwide provides education, consulting, and coaching to small business owners worldwide. Prior to founding E-Myth Worldwide, Michael launched a speed reading product and a stock photography company which he sold door-to-door.

INTERVIEW

Q: What was your initial startup cost and source?
A: Our first client invested $25,000 to help get the business started.

Q: How long until you had reached a positive cash flow?
A: 6 months.

Q: Did you use a business plan?
A: No.

MICHAEL GERBER

Q: What was the genesis of the idea?

A: A friend asked me to visit a small business (a small high-tech company) which was struggling to convert leads into sales. In that first meeting, I discovered a truth that he wasn't able to see. That truth led to the realization that most businesses are broken and a more creative approach is often needed. In that case, it was simply a matter of finding an uncommon answer to a common problem (why businesses fail). At E-Myth Worldwide in 1977, we had commission only sales people on the street filling seats in our seminars. It wasn't until 1984, when a woman we had hired insisted her fiancé attend one of our seminars. Her fiancé was a publisher at a subsidiary of Harper Publishing and suggested I put the material from the seminar into a book. I said OK, and they came back with a proposal and the rest is history. The book is actually the script for the seminar we had already been running for years.

Q: What came first, the problem or the solution?

A: It was in the moment that I finally saw the problem, that the solution immediately arose. Simply stated, it's how to design a scalable business. Failure of small business is the single biggest problem in the world. If we could make all small businesses successful, we could address all the world's problems.

Q: What is the passion that it fills for you personally?

A: I am on a mission to create a transformation of small business worldwide. I revel in seeing the success of the companies we work with. I enjoy inspiring and teaching others before they make the biggest mistake in their life. It's also challenging to design and run a company as though you were going to franchise the business. Unfortunately, most of what you hear in the world today is B.S. There is indeed a streetwise way to build and run a successful business and I feel an urgency to help other people see the truth.

Q: Where do you see yourself and your company in 10 years?

A: I'm 72 years old, and I have no desire to retire. I feel I am on a mission to fix this problem called the failure of small business. There is an urgency to solve what I see as the biggest single problem in the world. My companies are destined to

E-Myth Worldwide®

solve that problem and I'm determined to get a leg up on it between now and the day I pass.

Q: Looking back now, is there anything you wish you had done differently? What have been your biggest challenges?

A: The biggest challenge is people. Most people are looking outside themselves for the answer. The excuse to most people is always external. The entrepreneurial mindset however is always internal. It's people's inability to accept the fact they don't know the answer. There are very few great students in the world; people who are truly open and accept that they don't know everything. There is so much resistance to the truth of what I teach. People's egos can't handle it and too much determination in the wrong direction can be a significant fault. I don't live in the space of regret, but I suppose I would have financed my company differently vs. bootstrapping it. Bootstrapping is hard, but does teach you extraordinary lessons.

> *"Most people are looking outside themselves for the answer."*

Q: What have been your biggest rewards?

A: Watching the positive impact I've had on people whose lives and businesses were broken and had given up hope when we first met them. It was rewarding when they finally asked for help, discovered E-Myth, and made miraculous transformations. I never would have imagined that my books and my companies would be as successful as they've been or that I'd be labeled as the *World's #1 Small Business Guru* as recently stated by INC. magazine.

Q: Are there one or two things you can attribute your success to? Luck, timing, someone who helped you?

A: I attribute a lot to my earliest teachers, my saxophone teacher, my encyclopedia sales manager, the man who taught me how to build and frame a house. As a result of what my teachers taught me, I've been able to see a pattern in business that nobody else saw and articulate it in a way others could not. The answer also came from Ray Kroc (the founder

MICHAEL GERBER

of McDonald's), Howard Schultz (the founder of Starbucks); entrepreneurs who saw the business as a scalable system. They all had an idea bigger than anyone else had ever conceived. The truth is that E-Myth Worldwide is built upon the exact principals in my books. It's no surprise that we are an exemplar for our students and the very material that we produced. In short, we do E-Myth; we don't just talk about it. When hiring at E-Myth Worldwide, we teach people who know nothing about business how to become the very best business coaches, business salespeople, and business mentors possible using our expert system.

Q: How do you attract and retain the best employees?

A: In the early days, we attracted people on straight commission; everyone in the company was on 100% commission. What attracted people to our company was our dream – the idea that if we could transform small business worldwide, we could transform the world. That idea and that commitment have continued to this day. The people who are attracted to us are not attracted to doing the work; they're attracted to the impact the work we do can have on countless people throughout the world. In short, they're attracted by the dream, they're moved by our vision, they're committed to our purpose, and they're determined to become exemplars in implementing our mission.

Q: Can you recommend any training or resources such as books, classes, or websites? Do you recommend an MBA?

A: No on the MBA. Rather, I recommend a MBD – a Masters in Business Design, which is a new degree I'm creating. The first and only business book I ever read was *Marketing for Business Growth* by Theodore Levitt of Harvard University. It was the inspiration for E-Myth. I strongly encourage people to take our courses, read our books, and adopt our systems at E-Myth Worldwide.

> *"When people don't want to come, nothing in the world will convince them until you give them a different point of view."*

Q: Slogans to live by or what it might say on your tombstone?

A: "Never Quit." "It isn't what you know, but what you are determined to do that makes the difference. Knowing actually gets in the way." "When people don't want to come, nothing in the world will convince them until you give them a different point of view." That's what we have done at E-Myth. That's what I have been doing all my life – giving people a completely different point of view that transforms the way they think and because it transforms the way they think it absolutely transforms what they do and how they do it. But, "Never Quit" is key. It's in every message we give. It's in every mentoring we do. It's in every coaching relationship. "Never Quit, Never Quit, Never Quit." So obviously what's important as a part of all this is that you're absolutely dedicated to the 'great result' you're there to produce in the world. That's why I focus on the great result which is what the 'dream' is all about. The dream is the great result. The vision is the great how. To produce that great result the purpose is the great who. Who are you going to produce that great result for and why? The mission is the getting on with the delivering and developing the systems absolutely essential for building the capability to deliver that great result. "Never Quit, Never Quit, Never Quit."

Q: Anything else?

A: Creativity is counterintuitive. The things you need to learn are already within you. When you talk to others, keep in mind that they're usually going to give answers they're conditioned to give. The new entrepreneur I speak about in this age of the new entrepreneur that I talk about continuously, are finding uncommon answers to common problems. For examples of this, look at companies like Grameen Bank, McDonald's, Wal-Mart, and Starbucks. "Imagination", Einstein said "is more important than knowledge", and exactly as Nike said, "Just Do It."

> "The new entrepreneur that I talk about continuously, are finding uncommon answers to common problems."

"It takes great courage for men and women to discover their calling. After all, it may not be what you are doing now, and to face your calling squarely may cause some significant disruption in your life."

- from the book Prioritize by Joe Calhoun and Bruce Jeffrey

*"It's only when you have the courage to
step off the ledge, that you realize you've
had wings all along."*
Gail Lynne Goodwin, Inspire Me Today™

◆

BACKGROUND

Gail Lynne Goodwin began Inspire Me Today™ in 2008. Inspire Me Today™ is an Internet company offering inspiration through multiple forms of multimedia to people all across the world every day! Inspire Me Today™ utilizes only independent contractors and the startup cost was approximately $100,000. Gail's past entrepreneurial experiences include owning a real estate investment firm, a clothing company, and a record label in Nashville.

INTERVIEW

Q: Did you use a business plan?

A: No, I'm a firm believer that business plans limit you. While you should have an end goal in mind, you need to remain open on how you'll get there. That being said, if I need to borrow investment capital, then I'd write a business plan for that purpose.

Q: What was the genesis of the idea?

A: I've always pursued that which inspires me. I originally came up with the concept of Inspire Me Today™ in 2004, when I realized something about my daily workouts. I always listened to either inspirational/self help tapes or music. On the days in which I listened to inspiration, my entire day was incredible and I not only felt particularly good, but I was accomplishing more. It wasn't until 2006 that the idea resurfaced and I realized the impact it could have on the world. I was in Iraq touring military bases with my daughter when one soldier asked me for a "mom hug". He hadn't had a hug for nine months. He had been in the trenches for 37 days straight. I shared with him that I couldn't live in my house for a month with no contact with others and I asked him how he made it through that experience. He pulled out his iPod and told me, "everyday I listen to something inspirational on this, and it gets me through". I now offer our service free of charge to anyone with a .mil email address because of that experience.

> *"Being able to step away from the day-to-day 'drama' of life and maintain that focus is what determines success."*

Q: What is the vision of your company?

A: To provide the best inspiration daily to the world. We want to help people reconnect to the magnificence that they really are. I see myself as an ambassador of inspiration, gathering the best content. It's important to me that we offer a constant source of variety and thought provoking insights to our subscribers.

Q: What is the passion that it fills for you personally?

A: If you do what you love and love what you do, you'll never work another day in your life. This is my passion- bringing inspiration to the world. I get to do what I love, That is my wish for everyone.

Q: Where do you see yourself and your company in 10 years?

A: I can see the day that Inspire Me Today™ is a household name, and THE place that everyone turns to for daily inspiration. I see an empire like *Chicken Soup for the Soul!*

Q: Biggest challenges? What do you know now, that you wish you'd known sooner or at least handled differently?

A: Each day we've had challenges with things like the website not being where we want it to be, but maintaining the original vision is what keeps me going. I look at setbacks as becoming blessings in disguise. When the vision is big enough, it will get you past your fear. Being able to step away from the day-to-day drama of life and maintain that focus is what determines success. You have to maintain your original vision no matter what drama is happening at the moment.

Inspire Me Today™

Q: Biggest rewards? What aspects of ownership are the most rewarding? Any unexpected rewards?

A: You get to follow your passion and your dream, not someone else's. I'm also touched by the difference we're making in people's lives through our inspiration, and that's so rewarding. An unexpected reward was also the experience of helping my daughter fulfill her dream of becoming a recording artist. I created a record label in Nashville to launch her career. Willie Nelson even sang the duet, Crazy, on her debut CD. We spent two amazing years traveling around military bases entertaining troops and their families with her song, 'Baby Come Back Home'. As an entrepreneur, you get to create your own fun! You get to have all the freedom and flexibility you can create.

> *"Can't is not in my vocabulary, the word has no meaning to me."*

Q: Are there one or two things you can attribute your success to?

A: *Can't* is not in my vocabulary, the word has no meaning to me. Curiosity, I have a never-ending passion for learning and discovering what I don't know. I believe that the quality of your life is determined by the quality of your questions. Having good mentors and a willingness to ask for help. To be vulnerable and admit that I don't know the answer. Allowing others to help me, once they've caught the passion, and letting them run with the idea. Learning how to turn adversity into opportunity is also critical. But, the single most important thing is starting each day with gratitude, no matter what's going on in your life. Don't start your day without gratitude.

Q: How do you attract and retain the best employees? What is the most important attribute you look for?

A: I've done all my recent hiring on *craigslist.com* and only hire independent contractors, not employees. I look for the right attitude and a strong willingness to learn. The best indication that I've found the right person, is when I see they are having fun doing what needs to be completed.

GAIL LYNNE GOODWIN

Q: Do you recommend any books, classes or websites? Do you recommend an MBA?

A: As for websites, I strongly recommend *www.InspireMeToday. com* to start your day each morning. We'll brush the dust off of your wings and help you fly higher. We'll also connect you with entrepreneurs like Michael Gerber, John Assaraf and so many more, that can give you invaluable information. As for the MBA, don't think that having letters behind your name will automatically bring you success. I feel it is almost diametrically opposed to the mindset you need to have as an entrepreneur. Life is about going out there and just doing it. For books, I recommend *The E-Myth* by Michael E. Gerber, *Screw It, Let's Do It* by Richard Branson, *The 4-Hour Work Week* by Timothy Ferriss, *The Answer* by John Assaraf and of course, *www.InspireMeToday.com*.

> *"The single most important thing is starting each day with gratitude, no matter what's going on in your life."*

INSPIRE ME TODAY™

"He was an honest man."
Miles Grant, Genesis Homes

◆

BACKGROUND

Miles Grant founded his real estate development company, Genesis Homes, located in Littleton, Colorado in 1998. The company finds land that other builders have rejected, transforming it with new excavation technology to make it usable for housing. Miles, along with his seven employees, is able to connect home builders and home buyers throughout Colorado. The newest company venture is providing affordable housing to active adults. In the future, Miles sees his company focusing on senior single family homes built green to provide zero utility costs. His prior experience was as the President of Centex and Daly Homes.

INTERVIEW

Q: What was your initial startup cost and source?

A: My initial startup cost was $3 million from a syndication of partners, angels, and private placement.

Q: How long until there was a positive cash flow?

A: Two years.

Q: Did you use a business plan?

A: Yes, and I used business planning software.

Q: The genesis of the idea?

A: I bought a piece of land overlooked by the big homebuilders. I took a new technology of excavation to make the land usable for building. I basically saw a unique opportunity and jumped on it.

MILES GRANT

Q: The vision of the company and the community you serve?

A: The vision is to find land that other builders won't touch and make it usable. We serve the community by connecting home builders and home buyers throughout Colorado. Our new venture is providing affordable housing to active adults.

Q: The passion that your business fills for you personally?

A: Entrepreneurial independence. The company I worked for was beginning to compromise, and while I had entrepreneurial freedom most of my years there, the culture was beginning to change.

Q: Where do you see yourself and your company in 10 years?

A: We are building affordable green senior single family homes with zero utility costs. Our buyers may already be on a fixed income, and our homes allow them stabilize at least the utility aspects of their income.

Q: The biggest challenges?

A: Growing too fast; keeping control of the vision; having partners who influence me to buy more than I want to; cash flow and being in debt.

Q: The biggest rewards? Any unexpected rewards?

A: The occasional real big successes and associated payouts. There have been a few unexpected big profits I didn't anticipate.

Q: Are there one or two things you can attribute your success to? Was it luck, timing, or someone who helped you?

A: Look for diversity in everything you do. Diversify your vision. Diversity allows you to weather the down cycles, and every business has them. Luck and timing always help a little. We learned how to cut house build times to 90 days by changing the traditional build sequence. We are constantly reinventing ourselves based on new technology and new information. Always listen to the guys who've been doing it the longest.

> *"Diversity allows you to weather the down cycles, and every business has them."*

GENESIS HOMES

Q: How do you attract and retain the best employees? What is the most important attribute you look for? What are your thoughts on the employee-ownership model?

A: Look for people who accent your weaknesses. Systems are important to maintain honesty. Have a solid mission statement. Yes on employee ownership, and give them an opportunity to buy in. I offer to match my employee's investment. Think about what happens to the company if you die. Being listed as a key man on your insurance policy will save your company, and your employees deserve it.

> *"I used to spend a lot of time interviewing with other builders for a job, but what I was doing was learning their secrets."*

Q: Can you recommend any training or resources? Do you recommend an MBA?

A: I learned most of what I know about this business while I was working for a large corporation. I do recommend an MBA, however be sure you have a focus first. I have what might be called a "working MBA"; experience in the industry is key. Learn from other's mistakes. I used to spend a lot of time interviewing with other builders for a job, but what I was doing was learning their secrets. I've taken their best practices, and built a system around them.

Q: Slogan to live by or what it might say on your tombstone? What are your strongest core beliefs?

A: "He was an honest man." Honesty gives you a clear conscience, and your business will do well. Always follow through on your word; integrity is key. Lincoln was my hero.

Q: Is there anything else you want to share with an aspiring entrepreneur?

A: Being able to recognize great technology and great practices, then learning to implement them in a creative way, defines entrepreneurship.

MILES GRANT

"Man cannot discover new oceans unless he has the courage to lose sight of the shore."

- Lord Chesterfield

"Everything is going to work out"
Thomas Harvey, Dr. Thomas Harvey, DDS

◆

BACKGROUND
Dr. Thomas Harvey established his dentistry practice, Dr. Thomas Harvey, DDS in 1976 in Fort Collins, Colorado. Dr Harvey had no prior business experience and now employs four people. His initial startup cost was $50,000 which he borrowed from the bank.

INTERVIEW
Q: How long until positive cash flow?

A: Five years, namely because Fort Collins was fairly saturated. It was a very competitive market to enter. Six people from our class came here, and the existing dentists didn't want more local competition.

Q: Did you use a business plan?

A: No.

Q: The genesis of the idea?

A: My brother was a dentist and our family friend was a dentist. I didn't want the responsibility of a medical practice. I enjoy working with my hands and I love tinkering.

Q: The vision of the company and the community you serve?

A: I'm here to serve the people. There is no formal vision like a typical business.

Q: The passion that it fills for you personally?

A: Working with people. I always had great experiences as a kid going to the dentist, I was never hurt. I want to make the experience as pleasant as possible for my patients.

Q: Where do you see yourself and your company in 10 years?

A: Retired! Having sold off the practice to someone else.

Q: What were your biggest challenges?

A: I recall only 4 hours being spent on the topic of business in dentistry school. Getting started on my own, things were lean in the beginning (little cash flow). Finding new clients was a challenge. Back in the 1970's, things were a lot different in this profession and you were not allowed to advertise. You were only allowed to put a small office opening advertisement for the first two weeks after you opened your practice. We got creative and ran our ad for one week when we first opened, and ran the second week six months after we opened. The other dentists in the area were irate with us. Today things are much different. Having a business acumen is vital to having a surviving practice!

> *"As an owner, you have to be willing to do things an employee isn't willing to do."*

Q: What aspects of ownership are the most rewarding?

A: You get to pick where you want to live. Nobody tells you where you can make a living. You can set your own hours. You make your own decisions about your life. My patients are the biggest reward.

Q: Are there one or two things you can attribute your success to? Luck, timing, someone who helped you?

A: Time passing (patience) has really made the biggest difference. When times were tough, I was fortunate to have some financial resources to help pull me through. For a few years I had to set up a satellite office 100 miles away just to get enough business. I interviewed dentists in the area while I was still in dentistry school.

Q: How do you attract and retain the best employees? Any thoughts on the employee-ownership model?

A: I believe in treating everyone like equals. I prefer to spend my day in our common room, and not in my office. Everyone

Dr. Thomas Harvey, DDS

is equal and has equal say in decisions. I see my employees as partners. In medical professions, you can't have multiple owners.

Q: Slogan to live by or what it might say on your tombstone?
A: "Everything is going to work out," and "They only got what they needed."

Q: Anything else to add?
A: As an owner, you have to be willing to do things an employee isn't willing to do. Today, there is a quandary around over-treatment. It's a conflict of interest when you see doctors making a lot of money. It comes down to the ultimate question, "can you go home and sleep at night?"

THOMAS HARVEY

"Destiny is not a matter of chance; it is a matter of choice. It is not a thing to be waited for; it is a thing to be achieved."

- William Jennings Bryan

15

"He went for it!"
Bill Hibbler, Gigtime Media

◆

BACKGROUND

Bill Hibbler is one of the early pioneers of internet marketing. He is the owner of Gigtime Media and a dozen other domains including *EcommerceConfidential.com* and *RudlReport.com*. Bill first turned to the internet to help him market a seminar aimed at helping musicians manage the business side of their careers. Bill is the author of *Meet and Grow Rich: How to Easily Create and Operate Your Own "Mastermind" Group for Health Wealth, and More*, and *The Ultimate Guide to Creating Moneymaking Ebooks*, both of which he co-authored with Dr. Joe Vitale. Prior to starting Gigtime Media, Bill was a limousine driver in New York. It was that experience that convinced him to avoid the corporate world at all costs. Gigtime Media is currently run out of his home office in Wimberley, Texas. When Bill was just 15 years old he started selling vintage guitars, which evolved to include rental of sound equipment which eventually led him into the music business. Here he worked his way up to becoming a tour manager for some big names including Humble Pie. Bill just launched *AffiliateU.com*, a site that offers step-by-step lessons and tools to help people make money by tapping into internet marketing. It promises to be the ultimate source for everything you need to be successful online.

INTERVIEW

Q: What was your initial startup cost and source?

A: $2,000, credit cards. The majority of my investment went into buying Corey Rudl's training materials on how to get started in internet marketing.

Q: How long until you had reached a positive cash flow?

A: One year.

BILL HIBBLER

Q: Did you use a business plan?

A: Yes, but I felt it was one of the biggest waste of time looking back. Any long-range planning in our business is pointless. The game of internet marketing changes too fast.

Q: The genesis of the idea?

A: After years of being an artist and tour manager, I began teaching seminars to teach musicians about how to manage the business side of their careers. The problem was I was marketing my seminars to people who didn't have the money (the musicians) or the people who had the money but didn't have the talent. I began intensely studying marketing in an effort to get more people signed up. Early on I realized the importance of offering a product people need vs. a product they simply want. The trick in marketing is to find the market that needs (and can afford) your product or service. Internet marketing is all about tapping into needs that people are looking for but can't find anywhere else. It all started on eBay. I knew that a lot of people were looking for used copies of Corey Rudl's materials. So I started out buying low and selling high, and for a time it was fun to make $20 or $30 per sale. But what was beginning to happen was that I was becoming the expert on Corey Rudl's content. People would come to me before they laid down $2,000 or $3,000 for his courses asking for my opinion on which ones were worth it. I got a wild idea to put my own ebook up on eBay. I wrote a convincing sales letter and put up three eBay auctions with a $10 'buy it now' price. Keep in mind at the time I put the auction up, I hadn't even written the eBook yet! It was more of an experiment to see if anyone would buy it. Within 45 minutes, all three sold and I sat down that night to write my first eBook. I put up another three auctions the next day and they sold, and the next day, and the next day, and realized that I had tapped into a unfilled niche which had plenty of demand.

Q: The vision of the company and the community you serve?

A: My vision is to end unemployment by providing people a path to self-employment. For anyone who has a job they can't stand, to give them the tools to live their dreams and

GIGTIME MEDIA

pursue their passions. To help others avoid getting ripped off by false promises. To teach people the ropes of internet marketing as a way to either supplement their income or make it a full time job.

Q: The passion that it fills for you personally?

A: To help others find out what they are most passionate about and see the fulfillment in them that comes from it. When I left the music business, I was looking for people to connect with. The internet provided that vehicle for me. I want to be the mentor for others that I never had. Helping others find their freedom and live their dreams. Seeing people unhappy in their jobs and helping them discover a way to break free.

Q: Where do you see yourself and your company in 10 years?

A: I have no idea. I couldn't even begin to guess. One thing is to maintain having the ultimate freedom I enjoy now and continuing to help others do the same.

Q: Looking back now, is there anything you wish you had done differently?

A: My startup costs would have been a lot lower if I had looked for Corey's material on eBay first. But I have no regrets because had I not gone down the path I did, I would not have discovered the model I did. I would have started building my subscriber list sooner.

Q: Biggest rewards?

A: Connecting with others, especially at a personal level. In 2004, I wanted to spend a long weekend on the Riverwalk in San Antonio with my wife. My wife did not want to go, convinced that we not could afford the trip. I made a 'limited time' offer that weekend to sell all six products (remember I was in early on the affiliate game, so they were not all my own products) for only $97. It was a deep discount compared to what I normally sold the products for. I can't explain the sincere joy that came from watching all those orders stream in over the weekend while we more than covered the cost of the trip to San Antonio. I kept the game fun by keeping in touch with my customers throughout the weekend.

BILL HIBBLER

Q: Are there one or two things you can attribute your success to? Luck, timing, someone who helped you?

A: My grandfather owned a restaurant where I grew up. Everyone knew who he was, and no matter where we went, people would always come up and say hello. It was all about his personal relationships with others. Because my father was also an entrepreneur, I saw early in life the advantages of being the owner vs. being an employee.

Q: How do you attract and retain the best joint-venture (JV) partners?

A: A lot of people ask me to promote their products, but the only ones I work with realize that it's not about their product at all, it's about the personal relationship with them. My advice to others has always been to find out everything you can about the person whom you'd like to do a JV with. If you can appeal to that them personally first, you'll get a lot further in having them consider doing a JV with you. Find a way to connect with others on a personal level first.

Q: Can you recommend any training or resources such as books, classes, or websites? Do you recommend an MBA?

A: No on the MBA. I do wish I had stuck in college a little longer (I dropped out), but I do believe that college is more applicable for those who want to be an employee and get a job. Recommend books: *Think and Grow Rich* by Napoleon Hill. I know successful people who have read it over 100 times. My book, *Meet and Grow Rich* which expands the concept of mastermind groups mentioned in *Think and Grow Rich*. Mastermind groups have made all the difference. Even informal impromptu masterminds can be helpful. Also, *The Attractor Factor* by Dr. Joe Vitale is great to expand your mind to all the possibilities that exist in the world. It was through Jay Abraham that I discovered Corey Rudl.

Q: Slogan to live by or what it might say on your tombstone?

A: "He went for it!"- Face problems head on, fulfill on your dream, and go for it!

BILL'S TIPS FROM THE TRENCHES

1. One thing about ideas I've learned over the years is this: If nobody else is already doing it, it's going to be a lot harder to get your idea off the ground.

2. Competition is a good thing when you are able to see the value in joint ventures.

3. Relationships are the key. Evidence of this is the five figure publishing advance I received as a first time author (all because of my relationship with Dr. Joe Vitale).

4. People are more likely to learn from what they observe you do than what you tell them to do.

5. Regarding our current economy; the water may be rough for a time but it's up to you if you sink or swim. You can struggle to stay afloat, you can drown or you can view this as an opportunity to build muscle, grow stronger than ever and cross an ocean. You always have a choice.

6. What I can say with certainty is this: when I'm willing to put skepticism aside, take chances and do what's suggested by people that have been down the path before me, amazing things happen.

7. Until you become willing to do whatever it takes, you'll never find success. Sometimes that willingness can be difficult to come by and it takes something drastic to spur us into action. Unfortunately, it's often desperation that spurs people to take action.

BILL HIBBLER

"Learning is about more than simply acquiring new knowledge and insights; it is also crucial to unlearn old knowledge that has outlived its relevance. Thus, forgetting is probably at least as important as learning."

- Gary Ryan Blair

16

"Don't climb the corporate ladder,
be the ladder that others climb."
Michael Hills, Hampden Warehouse Liquor Mart

BACKGROUND

Michael Hills owns and operates Hampden Warehouse Liquor Mart in Denver, Colorado along with his business partner Adam. They currently have 10 employees. Michael's past entrepreneurial experiences include a car detailing company in high school, a small liquor mart, and being a landlord. At 28 years old, Michael was the youngest entrepreneur I interviewed. He plans to have his newest project, a casino, open by June 1st 2009.

INTERVIEW

Q: How long did it take you until your business earned a positive cash flow?

A: Six months.

Q: Did you use a business plan?

A: I did, but a very basic plan.

Q: What was the genesis of the idea?

A: I was working for a wine distributor and had been watching the business for awhile. My business partner Adam and I, in an effort to find out how to make a living and work for ourselves, asked "What do we know how do to?". A liquor store was one of those ideas, and when the opportunity presented itself, we opened a small store. Then, we had a chance to acquire a well established failed business, and I jumped on it.

Q: How would you describe your business model? How do you keep customers coming back?

A: Well, the business premise is simple. We offer a great selection with great service, at a low price. We also host wine tastings once a week.

Q: What is the passion that your business fills for you personally?

A: The independence of owning my own business is huge. I might be able to make more money today working for someone else, but I am building equity in a business I own now. I also thrive on taking calculated risks. But for me, my drive is on setting a goal and achieving it, despite what others say. I really enjoy rebuilding broken businesses.

> *"I might be able to make more money today working for someone else, but I am building equity in a business I own now."*

Q: Where do you see yourself and your company in 10 years?

A: My next venture is a new casino! We are well on our way already, and within 10 years, I'll be the owner of a successful casino. Ongoing, I see myself owning more businesses as well as the land and property with it.

Q: What were your biggest challenges? Looking back now, is there anything you wish you had done differently?

A: Raising money has been the toughest challenge. It has been especially hard to raise money as someone who is young. I have faced much age discrimination and nay-sayers. Being in my 20's, nobody would take me seriously and they always assumed my businesses were owned by somebody else, like my father. I've learned now to do as much correspondence as I can before meeting someone in person such as a lender, a principal, a client, etcetera. I try to let my results speak for themselves, and in doing so, I have found I am able to overcome the age discrimination.

Q: What have been your biggest rewards? What aspects of ownership are the most rewarding?

A: The freedom. The kickbacks from suppliers for being the owner, like getting tickets to Denver Broncos games! It has opened a lot of doors to meet others and network.

Hampden Warehouse Liquor Mart

Q: Are there one or two things you can attribute your success to? Luck, meeting, someone who helped you along the way? Was there a breakthrough that really made the difference?

A: My dad was a very positive influence on me. Education was big for me, it taught me to think creatively and to solve problems. Finding a like minded partner, Adam, has been huge for me. Seeking risk, and seeing things as they really are, have helped me get to where I am today. The KISS principle, Keep It Simple Stupid, has also made a world of difference for me. I am a firm believer that businesses break because they over complicate themselves. I've found that the key to fixing these businesses is by returning

> *"...my partner and I held a 'distinguished dinner series' where we would take an entrepreneur out to dinner and pick their brains"*

to the most basic aspects of running a business and putting all of your focus there. Early in my career, my partner and I held a 'distinguished dinner series' where we would take an entrepreneur out to dinner and pick their brains and just learn from them. This proved to be very valuable, similar to what you are doing with this concept! We just didn't consider sharing the results of those meetings in a book like you are.

Q: What is the most important attribute you look for in an employee?

A: Learn what skills are needed before hiring. You learn what they are by doing the job yourself! Avoid hiring friends or family. Find employees who are trainable. Some of my best employees at the liquor store are those who work there as a second job. If they've held another job for a period of time, it shows loyalty which I feel is important. Being able to make critical decisions quickly is extra important. As a side note, having a good inventory tracking system is very important in any retail business to discourage employee theft.

Q: Any recommended training and resources? Books, classes, websites?

A: Just do it! Don't be afraid of the risk. Join organizations in

MICHAEL HILLS

your industry. For books, my best advice is to read biographies, but also read *Rich Dad Poor Dad* by Robert T. Kiyosaki and Sharon L. Lechter, *The Millionaire Next Door* by Thomas J. Stanley and William D. Danko, *The Richest Man in Babylon* by George S. Clason, and Ayn Rand's *Atlas Shrugged*. *Atlas Shrugged* is like a modern day capitalist's bible. Everyone should read it!

Q: Do you recommend an MBA?

A: I don't feel an MBA is at all necessary. Street smarts are far more valuable, but you should definitely hire MBA's!

Q: Slogan to live by or what it might say on your tombstone?

A: Don't climb the corporate ladder, be the ladder that others climb. Work hard, play harder.

Q: Any last words or piece of advice?

A: Have fun with yourself and others. Don't take life so seriously. For example, I have had plenty of fun with my profile on LinkedIn! Don't get attached to things. As an entrepreneur, you have to be willing to tolerate pain.

MICHAEL'S TIPS FROM THE TRENCHES

1. Be involved in organizations and networking events.
2. Follow the KISS Principle: Keep it Simple, Stupid!
3. An MBA is important in your employees.
4. Don't take life so seriously.

17

*"Find something good in everyone, and help
them find it in themselves."*
Trina Hoefling, GroupONE Solutions

◆

BACKGROUND

Trina Hoefling, formerly a teacher, founded *GroupONE Solutions* in St. Louis, Missouri in 1984 before moving the business to Denver, Colorado in 1992. She helps business in the area of relationship management. Trina has built a niche around virtual companies with dispersed workforces. Her specialty is working with franchisors and closely held businesses, helping them establish the essential organizational structure for success. In 1994, she coined the phrase "expanding emotional bandwidth," as a way to help people connect across boundaries, knowing it was a concept valuable to businesses, but not realizing how significant that model would become. She believes that she is the "cause" in her life, and loves helping businesses become more successful, more easily, with less stress. Trina is also the author of several books and articles about working virtually.

INTERVIEW

Q: What was your initial startup cost and source?
A: Less than $18k, personal savings.

Q: How long until there was a positive cash flow?
A: 18 months.

Q: Did you use a business plan?
A: Yes, I use it as my strategic plan, and it is a constant work in progress.

Q: What is the vision of the company and the community you serve?
A: I help entrepreneurs in the area of relationship management. People need to manage three relationships – people to peo-

ple, people with technology, and people with the work itself. I've built a niche around virtual companies with dispersed workforces. I like to work with franchisors, ideally companies between 50 to 250 locations. I help them establish the essential organization structure for success.

> *"I realize now there is nothing wrong with self promotion and capitalizing on your brand."*

Q: What is the passion that it fills for you personally?

A: I love to help businesses become more successful, more easily, with less stress. I want people to enjoy the ride to the top, and am rewarded when I see them gain a new level of "clarity" that they were not able to see on their own.

Q: What was the genesis of the idea?

A: I and my partners started an outsourced telecommuting company in 1994. It was a concept that I knew was valuable to businesses. At the time, I did not realize how significant that model would become.

Q: Where do you see yourself and your company in 10 years?

A: Coaching other coaches. Working completely virtual, with more speaking engagements, and better leveraging the brand I've established for myself.

Q: Looking back now, is there anything you wish you had done differently?

A: I would have spent more time focusing on the forecast and profitability aspects of my business plan. I realize now there is nothing wrong with self promotion and capitalizing on your brand. In the past, I felt uncomfortable about what I viewed as "selling out" and spending time tooting my own horn, but now see there is nothing wrong with that, and it's in fact one of the smartest things you can do to sustain your livelihood. It's just about being smart in receiving value back for your efforts.

Q: What aspects of ownership are the most rewarding?

A: I love the freedom of my life now, and being able to do what

GroupONE Solutions

I love to do. And I am proud of the quality of the relation-ships I have with my business associates. I consider myself a life-long learner, and am never reluctant to ask for help, and because of this, never feel stuck any more.

Q: Are there one or two things you can attribute your success to? Was it luck, timing, someone who helped you?

A: My uncle Al was a big inspiration to me. He believed in me my whole life. I was the first college graduate in my family. I've always held the belief that I am the "cause" in my life, and will do whatever it takes to follow through on my com-mitments.

Q: How do you attract and retain the best employees? What is the most important attribute you look for?

A: Passion is contagious! I look for what becomes "collective creativity" in business partners. I am an advocate for em-ployee-ownership. Shared risks and rewards bring out the best in people.

Q: Can you recommend any training or resources such as books, classes, or websites? Do you recommend an MBA?

A: I suggest more focus on the arts. It helps spawn creativity, something businesses often lack. An MBA probably wouldn't hurt. As far as good books go, I like *The Leadership Pipeline* by Ram Charan, Stephen Drotter, and James Noel, *Guerilla Marketing* by Jay Conrad Levinson, and *E-Myth* by Michael Gerber. I'd also recommend any of my books, beginning with *Working Virtually*.

> *"I've always held the belief that I am the 'cause' in my life, and will do whatever it takes to follow through on my commitments."*

Q: Slogan to live by or what it might say on your tombstone?

A: "Find something good in everyone, and help them find it in themselves."

Q: Anything else, or other words of wisdom for the aspiring en-trepreneur?

TRINA HOEFLING

A: It's going to be hard work, but have fun and find balance in your life. You need to find a structure that works for you, and it'll likely be uniquely your own, but you need to find a way to get the important things done, including many things you won't want to do. Be disciplined and focused. Leverage the power of others to help you see where your own "leaks" are. Live beneath your means. Finally, have faith and confidence in knowing that you will get through the downturns. This is why failure is so valuable, it's evidence that you can survive adversity and setbacks.

> *"Have faith and confidence in knowing that you will get through the downturns."*

GroupONE Solutions

18

"Capitalism without conscience is greed."
Diane Hughes, Earth Friendly Coffee

◆

BACKGROUND

Diane Hughes is the founder of Earth Friendly Coffee (EFC) which she established in 2003. Diane currently has 4 employees and is a direct importer of organic, fair trade coffee. This is Diane's 3rd business and she previously worked at IBM for 16 years. Diane is a 'social entrepreneur', and her reasons behind EFC are genuinely altruistic. What impressed me most about Diane is how she knew absolutely nothing about the coffee business, but jumped in with both feet anyway and learned about the industry as she grew this business from scratch. She flew to South American on several occasions without a clear plan on who, what, or how she was going to go about it. There is a confidence about her that is unique, and I am seeing this similarity among many of the entrepreneurs I interview; they have an unbelievably strong faith that everything will work out fine (or perhaps the confidence that no matter what happens, they can persevere). Risk is something that holds many of us back from taking action. But I get the sense in talking to true entrepreneurs that yes, risk still exists, but it doesn't stop them from taking action anyway. It's a faith and optimism that things will work out , and if they don't, it doesn't have to deter them from trying anyway. They'll just make an adjustment and try again.

INTERVIEW

Q: What was your initial startup cost and source?
A: $50k, savings and credit cards.

Q: How long until you had reached a positive cash flow?
A: Three years.

Q: Did you use a business plan?
A: Yes.

Q: Have you had to morph your original business plan to meet the demands of the market?

A: Yes, many times.

Q: The vision of the company and the community you serve? Which came first, the problem or the solution?

A: EFC is a model social entrepreneur company, based on the belief that a business should not only be profitable, but positively impact society as well. In the case of EFC, the problem was identified first; that is that the coffee growers of Guatemala were being paid unfair prices by the large wholesalers and being forced to live in poverty. I established EFC to serve the needs of the indigenous people of Guatemala and as a direct importer I am able to pay the growers directly.

> *"Since the reason for the business in the first place was to help the Guatemalan people, I was able to connect with others who wanted to help me."*

Q: Where do you see yourself and your company in 10 years?

A: I'd like to take the business as far as I can and then sell all or a portion of it.

Q: The passion that it fills for you personally?

A: Making a difference by helping the indigenous people of Guatemala.

Q: The genesis of the idea?

A: On vacation, my husband Clancy and I were sitting in a café in Tulum, Mexico enjoying the most incredible cup of coffee and we were moved by the poor living conditions we saw and were inspired to find a way to help. I thought, "Everyone enjoys coffee, so why not bring this coffee back to the USA and insure the farmers are paid a fair price in the process?"

Q: Looking back now, is there anything you wish you had done differently? Any big challenges?

A: The biggest challenge is that we can only place one order per year - being sure I order enough, but not too much to meet

EARTH FRIENDLY COFFEE

demand. There has been a slower adoption to the fair trade movement among consumers than I expected. Employees; admittedly I tend to be too nice and managing employees is not my strength. Lastly, I should have explored the path of establishing EFC as a non-profit or hybrid non-profit.

Q: Biggest rewards?

A: EFC was the catalyst behind a government policy change in Guatemala, as EFC was able to show how the indigenous people of the region can thrive in the new world economy.

Q: Are there one or two things you can attribute your success to? Luck, timing, someone who helped you?

A: Since the reason for the business in the first place was to help the Guatemalan people, I was able to connect with others who wanted to help me. One person in particular who was extremely well connected and helped me make the vital connections I needed to get everything started.

Q: Any thoughts on the employee-ownership model?

A: I feel that an employee-ownership model that is performance based is a good idea.

Q: Can you recommend any training or resources such as books, classes, or websites? Do you recommend an MBA?

A: *Professional Selling Skills* (the curriculum that was originally developed by Xerox). I don't feel an MBA is necessary to be a successful entrepreneur. I'm a bigger fan of the school of experience.

Q: Slogan to live by or what it might say on your tombstone?

A: "Capitalism without conscience is greed." My strongest core beliefs are truth, honesty, and above all fairness.

DIANE HUGHES

"There is vitality, life force, energy that is translated through you into action, and because there is only one of you, your expression is unique. If you block it, it will never exist through any other medium and be lost forever. It is not your business to determine how good or valuable it compares with other expressions, it is your business to keep the channel open."

- Martha Graham

"Just jump in."
Brian Ibbott, Coverville Media, LLC

◆

BACKGROUND

Brian Ibbott started Coverville Media, LLC in 2004 after discovering a new technique to fulfill his dreams of becoming a DJ on a show that plays 100% cover songs, artists playing other artists' songs. Brian is one of the earliest pioneers of "podcasting." When his show is podcasted from his home studio in Arvada, Colorado, it is listened to by over 16,000 people around the world. In August of 2008, Brian celebrated his 500th episode by throwing a gala in Las Vegas. Fans of the show got to mingle with some of the artists featured on Coverville. Additionally, as a "podcaster for hire," he produces and hosts podcasts for other companies. Prior to Coverville, in the earliest days of the internet, he ran the website www.askbrian.com where he took pride in answering nagging questions that stumped people. Brian's advice to other entrepreneurs is to find a niche that you are passionate about. Then he suggests you "just jump in" because, "If you spend too much time on the edge of the pool trying to figure out how to do it, someone else will get there first."

INTERVIEW

Q: What was your initial startup cost?
A: Approximately $350 for a mic, mixer, website, and hosting.

Q: How long until there was a positive cash flow?
A: 4 months. My first sponsor came on board within 4 months.

Q: Did you use a business plan?
A: No.

Q: What was the genesis of the idea?
A: I was intrigued by what was referred to as an 'MP3 Blog' that

Adam Curry, the former VJ, was posting online. As the technology began to evolve, thanks in a large part to the open software movement, the possibility of having my own radio show emerged. My dream had always been to host an "all covers" radio show. The only resemblance of such a show was a short segment on satellite radio that no longer exists. As the technology of podcasting emerged, I jumped on my opportunity to get the show out there.

Q: What came first, the problem or the solution?

A: The solution came first, as a creative expression, second came the love of music, and lastly came the way to leverage the internet to broadcast a niche. It all integrates nicely into the world of podcasting.

Q: What is the passion that it fills for you personally?

A: I'd always been a wannabe DJ. I love music. I literally own thousands upon thousands of CDs. For a short time I was a wedding DJ, but it was not at all what I had envisioned. This is fulfilling my need for creative expression, tapping into my "music trivia mind," and providing entertainment to others.

Q: Where do you see yourself and your company in 10 years?

A: Coverville is a mainstream radio show, and I'm able to reach a much larger audience, that podcasting will likely never reach.

Q: What were your biggest challenges?

A: Learning the ropes on music licensing was a major challenge. Nobody had asked the questions before about how you get licensed to play entire songs on a podcast. I intentionally stay away from the major labels to avoid running into licensing problems. Bandwidth early on was a challenge as well. After Adam Curry mentioned me on his show, my subscriber base went through the roof.

Q: What are your biggest rewards?

A: The feedback from my listeners! The positive feedback from my listeners is the 'fuel' that makes doing this so much fun. I get emails from all over the world. I know my podcasts are

COVERVILLE MEDIA, LLC

being listened to, and talked about, because I see the evidence of it all the time. It has been a thrill to get mentioned in the media, including a text book, as a case study on new media,

> *"If you spend too much time on the edge of the pool trying to figure out how to do it, someone else will get there first."*

and Rolling Stone. One of my listeners shared with me that my show helped him through recovery from surgery. Artists now send me their CDs, and record labels approach me to have their artists on the show.

Q: Are there one or two things you can attribute your success to?

A: Getting in early as the technology was first emerging. In the beginning, there were only eight or so podcasts, so those of us in early had a fairly captive audience. Having numerous mentions on Adam Curry's podcast really helped. Timing and word of mouth have probably been the biggest factors.

Q: Any recommended books? How about an MBA?

A: No on the MBA. Two books I recommend on podcasting: *Podcast Solutions*, by Dan Klass and Michael Geoghegan, and *Podcasting for Dummies*, by Tee Morris and Evo Terra. A great book that I go back to time and time again is *Radio: An Illustrated Guide*, by Jessica Abel and Ira Glass.

Q: Slogan to live by or what it might say on your tombstone?

A: For a slogan: "Just jump in." For my tombstone: "A devoted husband and father." My family brings more joy to me than anything else, and I love being able to incorporate them occasionally into the show.

Q: Anything else?

A: First and foremost, do what you are passionate about. You do need to find a niche, but be sure it's something you are passionate about. Jump in with both feet, just get into it, and adjust later. If you spend too much time on the edge of the pool trying to figure out how to do it, someone else will get there first.

BRIAN IBBOTT

"The larger the problem you solve, the greater the rewards for solving it."

-Unknown

"What's next?"
Michele Isernia, Interclients

◆

BACKGROUND

Michele Isernia has been in and out of large corporations, in various countries, as well as cofounder of a few startups (Gear6, LogiSens and Interclients). For a chronology of Michele's career visit: *www.linkedin.com/in/isernia*.

INTERVIEW

Q: What was your initial startup cost and source of funding?

A: The startups I was involved in co-founding have always been self-funded, at least for the bootstrap phase. (Eight founders, five founders and two founders respectively). The first one Gear6 (ex Engineered-Intelligence) got multiple rounds of venture capital funding (as well as new products, new strategies and even a new name).

Q: How long until there was a positive cash flow?

A: In all three cases we never reached positive cash flow from sales.

Q: Did you use a business plan? If so, have you had to morph your original business plan to meet the demands of the market?

A: Yes, we always developed a complete business plan, which morphed multiple times.

Q: What came first, the problem or the solution? What is the vision of your company and the community you serve?

A: In the case of Gear6, the idea came first. Matt Oberdorfer, a brilliant German colleague, with whom I worked both in Europe and in the US, and the main founder of Gear6, invented something quite revolutionary and decided to build a com-

93

pany with a selected number of ex-colleagues.

With Logisens, the core technology was invented by Chris Stockinger, an Austrian engineer with a unique technology background; Chris as a person and his invention were interesting to me as the new company could make a positive difference in people's lives, something quite rare in many technology ventures.

Interclients, focuses on global business development for high tech and green tech products with partners in locations around the world (U.S., Europe and China), by leveraging the skills and relationships of a group of experienced individuals. All three companies had no relationship to the local community in Fort Collins. We did try very hard to connect to the community but we found it quite difficult.

Q: Where do you see yourself and your company in 10 years?
A: I keep my boundless curiosity alive and am always open to new ventures. I am much more balanced today and I believe I can find space for innovation inside companies of any size. I know I will always search for business opportunities that ignite a passion within, involve interesting and enjoyable people, and which can make a difference for the world.

Q: What was genesis of the idea? Was there a 'tipping point'?
A: In all my experiences, the core idea came from a core technology invention. The first "tipping point" is when you leave the dock and start sailing, leaving a secure job behind, with people you are not 100 percent sure about and with limited resources. Then, the definition of a startup is the hunt for the major "tipping point" that will turn a plan into a success (at least temporary). For people trying to figure out "the idea", I recommend paying close attention to activities you were involved at a young age at the times

> *"The first 'tipping point' is when you leave the dock and start sailing, leaving a secure job behind, with people you are not 100 percent sure about and with limited resources."*

when money wasn't the primary driver. The activities and passions you had from age 12 until perhaps 20-25 may reveal what you really love to do. Then, if you are so lucky, you will be able to make your true passions your business.

Q: What was your biggest challenge? Looking back now, is there anything you wish you had done differently?

A: Make 100 percent sure you are motivated to see it through and you have the capital (in your pocket) to survive at least three to four years. Also don't fall in love with the idea and don't get too attached to your business. I have seen people's lives destroyed because they become so engulfed in their business they sacrifice (and lose) everything along the way. There is a time when you must let go. Sometimes the game is over and it is time to move on. Find opportunities that have real market potential. Find novel ideas that are simple and easy for others to get. Be open to criticism, as consistent criticism from multiple people may contain some pearls of the hard truth (it is hard enough even for great ideas to succeed; so be humble and listen to feedbacks as they may

> *"The activities and passions you had from ages 12-25 may reveal what you really love to do. Then, if you are so lucky, you will be able to make your true passions your business."*

contain a lot of truth you are too blind to see). One of my personal learnings is that as the CEO you lose the right to truth. When you are the boss at the top of an organization, you will rarely ever get the full truth. Few employees are willing to take the risk and expose reality when things are not working to the one in charge (no matter how open, honest and non-threatening you may be).

Q: What are your biggest rewards? What aspects of ownership are the most rewarding?

A: The learning you get and lessons you learn along the way, the self confidence you carry in proving yourself, and discovering what you are really good at (and what you are not good

MICHELE ISERNIA

at). The most important unexpected reward is the ability to disconnect from the job you are performing and valuing yourself for what you really are, keeping a positive attitude in spite of the difficulties and failures. Another major learning is also born out of the many failures and how these shape your future.

Q: Are there one or two things you can attribute your success to? Was it luck, timing, someone who helped you, etc?

A: I do not consider myself "successful" in terms of my ventures being successful. I consider myself successful as I have learned a lot and will be able to do better in the next venture. I think that to be a great leader you must have failed at least once, as dealing with failure truly defines somebody's strength. (See Michele's *Tips from the Trenches* at the end of this interview for the factors he believes makes a company successful.)

> *"When you are the boss at the top of an organization, you will rarely ever get the full truth."*

Q: How do you attract and retain the best employees? What is the most important attribute you look for?

A: The question and the related answer are very different between a startup and a successful company. A good employee for a normal company may not have the skills to "survive and thrive" in a startup. And a "born entrepreneur" will probably die in 99% of corporations. Understanding what is behind somebody's motivation to join a company is very important because there may be 100 wrong reasons, and it will not last or it will not return value to the person and to the company. Surviving the bootstrap times in a startup is a very challenging experience for anybody.

Q: Do you have any thoughts on the employee-ownership model?

A: I have seen how the employee-ownership model can both help and hurt the business. It all depends how it is structured. I have found that offering shares in the company can be very difficult to manage and you can wind up spending

INTERCLIENTS

an unreasonable amount of time administering it, when you should spend all of your time on your product, your customers and your investors. It is also quite normal for people to change a lot during the first three to five years of a company life. Stock ownership creates unnecessary attachments to people that are no longer involved. At the same time, when there is little or no money for salaries, how do you reward people? This is incredibly difficult to balance; my learning is "keep it small" and do as much as possible with the smallest team, until you can afford paying salaries.

Q: Can you recommend any training or resources such as books, classes, or websites? Do you recommend an MBA?

A: Even though I have an Executive MBA from Stanford (I did it after 15 years of my career), I think that an MBA is not going to give you what you do not already have as far as personal skills, especially for leadership roles. I believe that the best and most important learning is based on direct experience. As far as sources for learning more, I see all of them as small opportunities to add to your own self, but nothing magical. Being open to new ideas, no matter the source, is always good and it contributes to form your mind further, but you are what you are and no book or reading will change that. Having said that, I do read a ton of books, magazines and internet sources, continuously.

Q: Slogan to live by or what it might say on your tombstone?

A: "What's next?"

Q: Is there anything else you want to share with an aspiring entrepreneur?

A: One simple and easy to remember analogy is the one of the 4 B's to determine if you are in the right job: Business, Boss, Bucks, Buddies. You should enjoy the business, have a good boss, make good bucks and like the buddies you work with. When you have all four of these satisfied, you are in the right job. You can deal with one of the Bs not working, but if more than one B is not working, it's time to move on. The specific drive to leave large corporations to take the major risk of starting new companies is born out of the limited space for true invention and innovation that is left in many large companies (see the book entitled *Innovator's Dilemma* by Clayton M. Christensen). For me, it was also somewhat "polluted" by the unrealistic expectations created by the Internet Bubble that made it seem easy. I worked for 17 years at Hewlett-Packard, in many different roles and locations around the world. I saw the company going from one of the most innovative companies in the world to a quite conservative and mostly operational money machine (great for the stock but poor for innovation). I started looking at start-ups as a way to be involved with innovation again. At that time, I remember visiting with a career counselor in Denver. The counselor posed the question; "at the end of your life, what would it take for you to feel that you're life had meaning?" The outcome of that conversation was to positively impact other people's lives. Finding a way to live that learning has been my constant strive; my greatest strengths, such as creativity, insight and the ability to inspire, and to appeal to what matters most to people, are still something I am always trying to find a "landing space" for.

> *"When you are the boss at the top of an organization, you will rarely ever get the full truth. Few employees are willing to take the risk and expose reality when things are not working to the one in charge."*

MICHELE'S TIPS FROM THE TRENCHES

1. **Simplicity:** If the product/solution is too hard to explain and understand, it will most probably fail or take a very long time to succeed. The smarter you are, the higher the risk.

2. **Focus:** The best companies understand their core skills and stay away from what they are not good at. Especially for a startup, be very conservative and stay small.

3. **Objectives:** Clearly defined and measurable objectives for the company, for the teams, and the people is the key to success. For many startups, where the direction can change multiple times, this is very difficult to manage, and requires a balance between involving and isolating the people doing the work from the brainstorming and strategy discussions.

4. **Motivation:** People and teams need compelling visions and reasons to go to work every day and keep up with the many difficulties that a new company encounters. If you start feeling weak in this area and cannot change it rapidly, it is time to move on (whatever that means to you).

5. **Find luck!** (Yes, you can "search" for luck...)

MICHELE ISERNIA

99

"It is better to follow the voice inside and be at war with the whole world, than to follow the ways of the world and be at war with your deepest self."

- Michael Pastore

21

"If you like what you are doing, you may never have to work another day in your life."
Jake Jabs, American Furniture Warehouse

◆

BACKGROUND

Finding the need and filling it has been the foundation of Jake's career. Jake Jabs began his entrepreneurial journey by purchasing a small guitar studio is Bozeman, Montana. It stemmed from the fact that he loved to play guitar (he used to play for Marty Robbins in Nashville), and that Bozeman lacked a music store with good guitars. When Jake sees an opportunity, he exemplifies the spirit of 'Carpe diem.' Twice, recessions have been the catalyst of his ventures – first in buying a struggling music store, then in buying a defunct furniture company. Today, Jake Jabs is the sole equity owner of American Furniture Warehouse (AFW), the largest furniture retailer in Colorado, which he founded in 1975. AFW has over 1300 employees and over $300 million annual revenue.

INTERVIEW

Q: What was your initial startup cost and source?

A: $80,000 I had saved. I bought the defunct American Furniture Company. They had over $1 million in assets on the books and wanted to get whatever they could for the old assets.

Q: How long until there was a positive cash flow?

A: 2 months

Q: Did you use a business plan?

A: No.

Q: What was the genesis of the idea?

A: In '74-75, Colorado was in the middle of a big recession. Lots of furniture stores went out of business and it looked like a great opportunity to get into a major market like Denver with a small investment.

Q: What is the vision of the company and the community you serve?

A: My vision was to sell furniture for less than anybody. We provide an opportunity for the community to buy furniture at a reasonable price and people love us because of that.

Q: What were your biggest challenges? Looking back now, is there anything you wish you had done differently?

A: I have no regrets in life and wouldn't change a thing.

Q: What have been your biggest rewards?

A: Having the ability to contribute to charities I believe in. I enjoy the opportunity to speak to high school and college students, as well as business groups.

Q: Are there one or two things you can attribute your success to? Was it luck, timing, someone who helped you?

A: Timing was key, buying a defunct company at the end of a recession when business started to pick up. Plain old fashioned hard work has been a vital key to our success. Being honest and up front with the customer has always been our core value, conveying the fact that furniture is not a perfect item. Although nothing is more costly that returns, I'd rather have the furniture back than an unhappy customer. Back in the 80's, we were really struggling, and on the brink of closing. But I worked hard to maintain impeccable credit and since I always treated suppliers as partners, they stood behind me during those difficult financial times. They would often give us a lower price than anyone else, even our competitors who were purchasing higher volume. What differentiates us and our competitors is that we rarely return damaged furniture to the supplier. Instead, we have a full time staff doing repairs, just as the supplier would have in their own factories, but doing it in our stores al-

> *"I was never in this for the money. To this day, I truly believe the result of my success has been due to the fact that I simply love what I do."*

lows us to save time and shipping costs.

Q: What is the most important attribute you look for in an employee?

A: We pay better than the other furniture stores and I give them freedom and responsibility to do their job. I spend an entire day with new employees. Doing so allows us to maintain a culture key to our success, to under-promise, over-deliver, and above all else, be honest with the customer. I also always try to first promote from within instead of hiring from outside.

Q: Any recommended training and resources? Books, classes, websites? Do you recommend an MBA?

A: No on the MBA. I use my own book, *An American Tiger*, as a training tool for our employees.

Q: Slogan to live by or what it might say on your tombstone?

A: If you like what you are doing, you may never have to work a day in your life.

Q: Anything else?

A: I was never in this for the money. To this day, I truly believe the result of my success has been due to the fact that I simply love what I do. That's why even at 78-years-old, I have no desire to retire. Money, for me, was never the motivation. It's more about the journey from a small guitar studio with two employees to a company now doing over $300 million with over 1300 employees. Money and happiness are not synonymous. I see a lot of people with plenty of money less happy than those without. The businesses that I've seen struggle, especially in times like now, with tight credit, are those that have overextended themselves. You need to focus on your liquid assets and not expand just for the sake of expanding.

Author's Note:
Be sure to check out *Appendix D* for Jake Jab's
35 Keys to Business Success.

"The quality of our lives is determined by the quality of our thinking. The quality of our thinking, in turn, is determined by the quality of our questions, for questions are the engine, the driving force behind thinking. Without questions, we have nothing to think about."

- Dr. Linda Elder and Dr. Richard Paul

22

"Find the win-win."
Mike Jensen, Fort Collins Real Estate

◆

BACKGROUND

Mike Jensen purchased Fort Collins Real Estate in Colorado in 2003. In September 2008, he merged with Keller Williams Realty, and currently has 36 employees. His focus is on urban infill redevelopment projects, mixed use development, and transit oriented developments, all with sustainable and green technology components. He always had the entrepreneurial bug, starting a lawn business when he was young. As a teenager he worked as a carpet cleaner and in the middle of the afternoon, when the landlord walked in wearing cutoffs and flip flops, Mike asked him "Shouldn't you be at work?" the answer was, "I am at work. I'm the landlord, this is what I do." This gave Mike an early glimpse into who he wanted to be. In 1996, continuing to work for FourStar while pursuing his degree at CSU in real estate and finance, he started his first company, Housing Helpers. It was a simple business model: find students who needed a place to rent, then find rentals or acquire the properties to rent to them. He grew the company from two employees to over fifty, and sold it in 2001 (just prior to 9/11). In addition to his various business successes, in only twelve years, he has amassed a personal real estate portfolio of over 150 properties valued at over $55 million.

INTERVIEW

Q: What was your initial startup cost and source?

A: Approximately $225,000, but because I had no money to start a company right out of college, and in fact I was over $28,000 in debt from student loans, I presented my business plan to Rich Taranow who financially backed the startup of Housing Helpers. The agreement was that I would give up 50% of my commissions for the first 100 transactions. Rich expected it would take me three to four years, but I did over

100 transactions within my first twelve months, and shortly thereafter bought Rich out.

Q: How long until there was a positive cash flow?

A: Immediately. In fact, I paid off my student loans within four months of graduating. I was closing on average eight to twelve deals a month.

Q: Did you use a business plan? If so, have you had to morph your original business plan to meet the demands of the market?

A: Yes. Absolutely!

Q: What was the genesis of the idea?

A: The idea was born before college. I worked for FourStar Realty and Property Management. I learned how they ran their business, and the idea of Housing Helpers. My last year of college I worked on a business plan to replicate what I saw at Fourstar; everything from managing properties to selling properties.

Q: What is the vision of the company and the community you serve?

A: For over 6 years, I've had this vision statement posted on my desk where I can see it every day: "Premier redevelopment, urban infill, and mixed use developer in Fort Collins. By aligning with parties who will hold and share similar interests/ visions possessing the wherewithal to implement the vision. Focusing on old town, the Poudre river corridor, areas surrounding Colorado State University, and in and around historically significant parts of Fort Collins. An emphasis on creating a cultural atmosphere that is friendly to residents, visitors, businesses, and varied lifestyles while being sensitive and responsible to the needs of our community and the preservation of our environment."

> *"I've learned that when you focus on the client and the deal they win too, and then the money follows."*

Q: What is the passion that it fills for you personally?

A: I'm a deal junkie. I like to win "the game." I've learned that when you focus on the client and the deal they win too, and then the money follows. When I was young, I remember Monopoly and Risk were my favorite games; and I was good at both of them. What I do today is even more fun than those board games were when I was a kid, but I still view business that way, as "a game." I'm passionate about making a real difference in the community and being recognized for it. For me the financial freedom is all about having time to do the things like coaching youth baseball, and volunteering for the community in which I live.

Q: Where do you see yourself and your company in 10 years?

A: I recently went through a divorce, and it really changed my thinking. My ex-wife said "you were cheating on me with your work." It's forced me to really re-evaluate how my business can run without me. Since we merged with Keller Williams, I've been able to adopt their model and systems. I hope to be financially positioned to have ample time and energy to focus on things away from work. For example, I recently started a non-profit, called *Cause Kids Count*, and I'd like to spend more time on it. I see the new company, Keller Williams, growing to over 500 agents from the 215 we have today.

> *"I wish I would have spent more time networking with people who were already doing it, and already where I wanted to be."*

MIKE JENSEN

Q: What were your biggest challenges? Looking back now, is there anything you wish you had done differently?

A: I probably would have done more outreach in terms of identifying best practices. There are so many ways, systems, and models you can adopt. I wish I would have spent more time networking with people who were already doing it, and already where I wanted to be. You need to have good controls in place. Finding enough capital is always a challenge. I always wish I could borrow more. You could sum it up like this: I do not regret the properties I bought, but the ones I did not. It is always a matter of having more money, not more opportunities.

Q: What have been your biggest rewards? Any unexpected rewards?

A: Recognition from others. People stop me on the street to tell me they appreciate the work I've done. I've found that people want to do business with the owner, and someone who is community minded. It is a huge credibility builder, especially when it comes to big ticket transactions like real estate.

Q: Are there one or two things you can attribute your success to? Was it luck, timing, someone who helped you?

A: You create your own luck. It takes hard work and perseverance to create luck. Timing in real estate is key; you have to know when to buy and when to sell. Having a clear vision; knowing what you want to accomplish in life. Knowing that we all have a limited amount of time in our life, and asking "what do we want to be remembered for?" Growing up as a kid I was the best at Monopoly, and I still am. There's a simple strategy to win: you buy everything you land on, mortgage everything, get the cash and continue to buy, and as the cash flow increases you buy more. The more you own, the greater your leverage, and your cash flow in turn increases. There is no limit to the creativity you can use to cut any deal to acquire more. Just remember there are always shortcuts, and winning is the goal of the game. In life and in business, you need to figure out what the "win-win" is; whether it is getting this deal closed, or being known as the place to go for downtown real estate. It's all about knowing your win, and doing whatever it takes.

> *"I do not regret the properties I bought, but the ones I did not."*

Q: What is the most important attribute you look for in an employee?

A: I've always believed in taking care of my people to build loyalty. The wrong employee is always looking for more than

I can give; the good employee can strike a balance. The more time I can spend interviewing up front, and following up

> *"In life and in business, you need to figure out what the 'win-win' is..."*

with their references, has been the most valuable. I look for a particular personality type, sometimes using DISC profiles (Dominance, Influence, Steadiness, Conscientiousness), and have found the most successful are those who have a driving need to get things done. To check things off their list right away. Tenacious to the point they are pushing me, and getting frustrated at having to wait for answers.

Q: Any recommended training and resources? Books, classes, websites? Do you recommend an MBA?

A: No on the MBA, but I don't have one, and a lot of the most successful entrepreneurs I know don't even have college degrees. Books: *Home Is Where the Boat Is* by Emy Thomas really changed my life. I'm an advocate for any books that help you keep your dreams alive. I'm always reading non-fiction, and I love books on strategy. I think there are lots of good ideas out there, and I'm always open to them. Right now I'm reading *Blue Ocean Strategy* for the second time, *Authenticity* by Joe Pine, *Green Office Buildings*, and *Strategies for Real Estate Companies*.

Q: Slogan to live by or what it might say on your tombstone?

A: Life is a negotiation. Live life to the fullest. Don't be afraid to dream. Don't be afraid to do anything and everything you want. Work hard, play hard. Find the win-win.

MIKE JENSEN

"If you want to move people, it has to be toward a vision that's positive for them, that taps important values, that gets them something they desire..."

- Martin Luther King, Jr.

"He did the best he could with what he had and had fun doing it"
Bill Johnson, Bill Johnson Enterprises

◆

BACKGROUND

Bill Johnson of Bill Johnson Enterprises established his newest company, Amazing Rake in Granite Bay, California in 2007. At age 22, Bill started working at Farnam Companies, a leader in the animal health care industry as one of five employees. Bill retired as President of Farman Companies fifty-three years later at age 75, having grown the company to over 350 employees. Bill is currently a motivational speaker, sales trainer, marketing wizard and serial entrepreneur. His current venture, Amazing Rake, with founding partner, Lyle Ethington, has three employees.

INTERVIEW

Q: What was your initial startup cost and source of funding?
A: $60,000 which was raised primarily through angel investors.

Q: How long until there was a positive cash flow?
A: Expected to be twelve months.

Q: Did you use a business plan? If so, did you have to modify the original business plan to meet the demands of the market?
A: Yes, the business flow occurred differently than we first envisioned so we have updated the business plan accordingly.

Q: What is the community you serve? What came first, the problem or the solution?
A: The problem, in that picking up leaves is hard due to constant bending over. With the Amazing Rake you never have to bend over! The market is anyone with a yard and leaves!

Q: What is the passion that it fills for you personally?

BILL JOHNSON

A: I enjoy making others feel good. I learned early in life that the more I gave, the more I got back. It is rewarding for me to see the people I've worked with do so good.

Q: What was the genesis of the idea?
A: Amazing Rake is a partnership with Lyle Ethington. Lyle and his original partner had a falling out and he kept all the rights to Amazing Rake through the settlement.

Q: Where do you see yourself and your company in 10 years?
A: Amazing Rake will likely be sold off to a larger corporation. We've already had many offers.

Q: What is your biggest challenge? Looking back now, is there anything you wish you had done differently?
A: We discovered that the material plastic is a world commodity just like oil. All countries pay the same price. We decided to keep manufacturing here in the USA since the savings to move production to China was minimal since there isn't a high labor component in production. I've also learned in all my ventures that doing lots of market research is essential. It's important to remember to slow down and do the research before investing your time and money. Cash flow and people are indeed the biggest challenges in any business. Business owners tend to be concentrated on their idea, not the workings of the business. This is the primary reason having a business plan is so vital! My only regret in life is not spending more time with my family.

Q: What is your biggest reward? What aspects of ownership are the most rewarding?
A: Taking a product that has been difficult for someone else to sell, and then being able to successfully market the product. Certain principles in marketing just flat work; finding a product, doing market research, finding out about the competition and then getting the product to the right tradeshows. I might publish a book I

> *"It's important to remember to slow down and do the research before investing your time and money."*

BILL JOHNSON ENTERPRISES

wrote for my twenty-four year old son someday.

Q: Are there one or two things you can attribute your success to? Was it luck, timing, someone who helped you, etc.?

A: If you can attract a crowd, you will be successful. Build yourself into the go to guy by always being willing to lend a hand and become friends with those who buy your services. Don't whine and complain. I've always been a hard worker putting in twelve hour days. Find some mentors and be open to learning from them. I caught the fever of winning early in my career and strived to hone my skills in the game of work.

> *"If you can attract a crowd, you will be successful."*

Q: How do you attract and retain the best employees? What is the most important attribute you look for?

A: I believe in offering up plenty of sweat equity in the beginning before asking for anything financially in return. When hiring, you have no way of knowing what their work ethic is, but after ninety days you'll know. Just because someone has a good track record doesn't necessarily mean they'll be a good fit in our company or with my personality. Over the years, I've found kids that grew up on farms have a very strong work ethic. The old joke is Farm is spelled w-o-r-k.

Q: Can you recommend any training or resources such as books, classes, or websites? Do you recommend an MBA?

A: Yes on the MBA, but get a four year degree. I read a lot of articles from business magazines such as *Inc., Fortune, Money* and *Entrepreneur*. I also read the business section of the newspaper regularly. I also read a lot of biographies; I try to study successful people and apply their techniques. I recommend reading the book, *The Greatest Salesman in the World* by Og Mandino.

Q: What is your slogan to live by or what might it say on your tombstone?

A: "He did the best he could with what he had and had fun doing it" and "Always lend a hand".

BILL JOHNSON

"Before you become unstoppable for others, you must become unstoppable for yourself."

- Unknown

24

"Let your life speak."

Kim Jordan, New Belgium Brewing Company Inc.

◆

BACKGROUND

New Belgium Brewing Company Inc. was founded in 1991 by newlyweds Jeff Lebesch and Kim Jordan. What originally began in 1985 as a home brewing hobby for Jeff has evolved into the third largest microbrewery in the United States, employing over 300 people. The core values and beliefs that Kim and Jeff originally built the company on are still in place today and have earned them the highest respect among their 300+ employee-owners. As the recipient of numerous awards – far too many to mention here – New Belgium is often considered the poster child of success and those of us who live in Fort Collins, Colorado are truly fortunate to have them in our backyard.

INTERVIEW

Q: What was your initial start-up cost and source?

A: $60,000 through a second mortgage on our house, and then we took some pre-approved credit cards for some operating capital along the way and maxed out all of our personal credit cards. That was just to start the business. We had a little money to live on in the bank, but nothing significant. We had credit cards.

Q: How long until there was positive cash flow?

A: You can have positive cash flow and still have debt, but we actually had cash flowing pretty well within six months of starting the company. We had enough cash flow to be able to begin to think about expansion, build a walk-in cooler and be able to do some of the things we needed to do. However, there was a period before we moved into our second location when we had so little cash flow that we had to borrow some money from my parents to make payroll. And we lived for about a year off of credit cards.

Q: Did you use a business plan?

A: Not in the beginning. But we did have a set of values, a purpose, and some outcomes that we wanted to achieve. They were more like guiding principles and objectives. With that said, a lot of work went into the diagrams for how the electricity was going to be wired up and how the tanks were going to be engineered and manufactured. But we had nothing in terms of a traditional business plan.

Q: The genesis of the idea?

A: Jeff volunteered at Sierra Nevada and took some classes on brewing at UC Davis. He then went to New Albion Brewing, which was really one of the first craft breweries in the US. He had also probably hung around the Boulder Brewing Company once or twice as a home brewer. In 1987 he started winning awards in national home brew competitions with his own beers. Then, in 1989, when Doug, Corky and Wynn opened Odell Brewing Company, we became friends and Jeff thought to himself, "If these guys can do it, then so can we" (Kim noted the highest respect for Doug, Corky and Wynn and this statement is not intended to be demeaning in any way). We just started putting the pieces together to make it happen. It was early in the development of the craft brewing scene, especially in Colorado, so we were able occupy the bottled beer niche that nobody else wanted to be in at that time.

Q: What was the vision of New Belgium?

A: Before we ever made a bottle of beer we sat down and asked ourselves what we wanted this company to stand for. The four things that were important to us then were to produce world class Belgium style beers, to promote beer culture, to be environmental stewards and to have fun. That was in the spring of 1991 and we started selling beer in June of 1991.

> *"It's just following your instincts, knowing the basics and sticking with what's important."*

NEW BELGIUM BREWING COMPANY INC.

By 1995, as we got more customers and coworkers, we expanded our vision to take their needs into account. We combined open book management, employee ownership (our coworkers own 32% of the company), and a high-involvement culture. Our coworkers get see all of our financials. They see all of our branding and sales plans. They see all of our CapEx plans, our hiring plans, our budgets, and our strategy – and they participate in developing them. Once you get everyone knowing where true North is, it frees people from uncertainty and allows them to do the more creative work. That way, powerful ideas come from all across the company: big ideas, little ideas, money saving ideas, and culture-building ideas. I think most people here would tell you they feel like their contribution matters and that is huge in and of itself. People want to feel that what they do matters.

Q: What is the passion that it fills for you personally?

A: I've been genuinely surprised and delighted to discover how much change you can make in business. There are some good reasons for people to be suspicious of profit motives and big corporate entities – especially given the recent AIG management news about their unwillingness to return taxpayer funded bonuses. But at the same time, you can do really powerful good work with profits. For us, that means talking about the big things that we want to do, the kind of things that get people on the edge of their seats, and being business role models. How can we change the industry we're in? How can we do things that will make both a splash and a ripple? How can we make an impact on the world that satisfies our internal sense of what's right? For example, we are doing a life cycle analysis of a six pack of Fat Tire. We're identifying where we can make changes both upstream and downstream in order to impact the environment and create a more sustainable industry.

> *"My biggest reward has been coming to understand how powerful we can be."*

KIM JORDAN

Q: Where do you see yourself & your company in 10 years?

A: We're really looking at whether growth is a matter of putting more barrels on the board or if growth is more about promoting our core values and beliefs, like love and excellence, and being role models for other businesses. And I would say we've come down more on the latter than the former. We're looking at developing relationships with smaller craft brewers around the US. The goal is to put together a network of brewers that can brew for one another so as to reduce our carbon footprint, be more local, and have hubs of smaller, more creative breweries. That's what I see New Belgium doing.

For me, I think I will probably continue to be involved ten years from now, at some level in the company. I might have moved into a chair role by then, as opposed to CEO. I'm cognizant of the fact that this has been an incredible gift and we're involved in a craft – so I want to remain a part of that. Of course, you never know where you will be. When the company was very young, Jeff was doing an interview with someone and he said, "Well, we've got this worked out where if we can make and sell 60 cases a week, then I think we can do this." We have that interview hanging up on a wall because we're so clearly past 60 cases a week.

Q: Biggest challenges? Looking back now, is there anything you wish you had done differently? What do you know now that you wish you'd known sooner?

A: It was originally a challenge to figure out how to provide enough opportunities for our fellow coworkers. We thought "Gosh, we have all of these dedicated and talented people – and if we don't grow then they won't have any opportunity and all of us are going to sit in the same chairs." It would have felt very stagnant. Growth by itself was never compelling. But that attitude all flipped when we started to see the opportunity for our coworkers.

In general, I don't know that there's anything I would have done differently because I think everything you do adds to both the mistakes and the successes – and you can't foresee either. When you're self-taught you think maybe there are experts out there who know a lot more than you know, and then you start to meet some of those people and you're not so sure. A lot of this is not some kind of mad intelligence. It's just following your instincts, knowing the basics and sticking with what's important.

Q: Biggest rewards, what aspects of ownership have been the most rewarding and have there been any unexpected rewards?

A: My biggest reward has been coming to understand how powerful we can be. As far as unexpected rewards go, I still have 'pinch me' moments. I walk in the front door on a Thursday afternoon and I just really can't believe this is our brewery. Being in this industry is a gift because people are so interested in what we're doing, and I don't want to squander it because I think the work is powerful and I want to spread that out in a smaller way. Another reward is watching our people grow into positions of more responsibility. I'm five to fifteen years older than most of my coworkers. Watching them get married, have children, grow into their professional life, and grow into their community involvement is both really rewarding and really fun.

Q: Are there one or two things you can attribute your success to? Was it luck, timing, someone who helped you, etc.?

A: I think luck and timing are always important, and working hard and being dedicated or committed to an outcome is key. That's how you get lucky: you have good timing and you work hard at it. At the time we put our vision together, we didn't realize that it was going to be as fundamental to who we are as it has been. That vision has been central to the choices we've made and to our success.

Q: How do you attract and retain the best employees? What is the most important attribute you look for, and your thoughts on the employee ownership model?

A: The most important attributes we look for are enthusiasm and dedication, which are slightly different but go hand in hand. I also think it is important to hire people who are drawn to a commitment to community. We want the gen-

KIM JORDAN

erally good people, who are decent human beings. But you can be all of those things and if you're still sitting on a couch all day, then none of those attributes are going to help. There has to be execution. We get a lot of things done around here.

Q: Any recommended training & resources? Books, classes, websites, etc..? Do you recommend an MBA for an entrepreneur?

A: We don't look for people with MBA's when we hiring. It is important to have the ability to read financial statements, understand ratios, and have a good overview of general HR legal policy – but you can learn all those things on the web or you can hire people to do them.

For books, *Beyond Entrepreneurship*, by Jim Collins, has helped us create a framework for our vision. *The Great Game of Business*, by Jack Stack, which is a book about open book management, is another good one. *The Leaders Handbook*, by Peter Scholtes, incorporates a lot of Dr Deming's thinking. It's about how to make sure that the systems and the communications you have are getting the results you want. The classic *One Minute Manager*, by Blanchard and Johnson, is helpful in knowing how to deal with what's going on quickly. We don't waste a lot of time.

I have also used business coaches and I'm sure I will use one again. Mastermind groups would probably be worth doing, but right now I feel like I'm so busy with other things that I'm more interested in one-on-one coaching.

Q: Slogan to live by or what it might say on your tombstone?

A: "We are right where we're supposed to be" – and when you think about that in terms of putting it on your tombstone, it's kind of amusing. I am also very fond of George Fox's saying, "Let your life speak."

Q: Is there anything else you want to share to an aspiring entrepreneur?

A: I think it's important to love what you do. It is not unusual to

NEW BELGIUM BREWING COMPANY INC.

work 15 hours a day at the beginning of any entrepreneurial venture. And if you don't love what you're doing, spending 15 hours a day doing it is very difficult to sustain for any length of time. It's not unlike raising a baby. In that early period, it takes a lot of dedication and nurturing, which is the equivalent of work. But, in anything you do, it is particularly satisfying when you figure out what feeds your soul and get that into the mix.

Eventually, babies move into childhood, get older, go to school and they begin to take less and less of your time. The same natural progression applies to a business. If you're still having dinner table conversations about work most nights and your business is older than five years old, then I'd say you haven't figured out how to balance those things.

KIM JORDAN

(Authors Note: A couple weeks after my interview with Kim, I ran into her at the airport, in one of the last places I would have ever expected: the shuttle bus from the $5 per day lot. I was shocked to see the CEO of a multi-million dollar company riding the bus from the cheapest lot in the airport. Nobody would have ever known that she parked there, to save money for New Belgium, and it struck me: it's what you do when people aren't watching that makes all the difference. Needless to say, I hold the highest regards for Kim Jordan and the New Belgium family. Oh, and in spite of being someone she had met only once, she remembered my name.)

"You will become as small as your controlling desire, or as great as your dominant aspiration."

- James Allen

25

"Every human being desires to work under a ceiling of authority."

Rich Kopcho, Holonyx

◆

BACKGROUND

Rich Kopcho is a serial entrepreneur who came out of retirement to launch Holonyx, a company focused on building technology solutions that meet the unmet needs of business today. Founded in 2007 in Loveland, Colorado, Holonyx currently has ten employees who work in the software as a service (SaaS) industry. This is Rich's fourth startup. He was an early contributor in two well known Colorado technology companies; Advanced Energy and Colorado Memory Systems.

INTERVIEW

Q: What was your initial startup cost and source?
A: $1.5mil (primarily self funded) and a lot of human capital.

Q: How long until you had reached a positive cash flow?
A: We are projecting positive cash flow in one year.

Q: Did you use a business plan?
A: Yes.

Q: Did you have to morph your original business plan to meet the demands of the market?
A: We've been using it as an internal roadmap to refine our business processes. We are still refining it.

Q: The vision of the company and the community or market you serve?
A: A holon is something that is simultaneously a whole and a part, a system that is a whole in itself as well as a part of a larger system. Holonyx is built on the premise that we are autonomous yet cooperative. It is the art of bringing the right

> *"Focus, people, and cash flow are the three biggest challenges."*

pieces together to create a whole solution. At its core, it is the science of architecting wholeness. We begin with consulting, then architect and build solutions around the needs identified during the consulting phase. At Holonyx we are able to offer our clients access to our three primary core competencies: Operations, Marketing, and Technology.

Q: Where do you see yourself and your company in 10 years?

A: To retire again. I know the company will morph considerably primarily into biotech (bioinformatics and grid computing and storage), but also in other areas where we identify 'veins of demand'. The goal is to mine new markets once we find the richest veins.

Q: The passion that it fills for you personally?

A: The sense of accomplishment, making things happen, and changing the face of tomorrow.

Q: The genesis of the idea, what came first, the problem or the solution?

A: Going back to one of my earlier startups (System II), I recall that it was a matter of addressing a need that our client couldn't get filled. No supplier existed, so we created it. In the case of Holonyx, it was the spark of an opportunity I saw partnering with a software solution company we purchased, Ruffdogs, which had created a number of products including RESTORE open-source backup.

Q: What were some of your biggest challenges?

A: Focus, people, and cash flow are the three biggest challenges. Focus: in picking one idea out of a thousand. People: particularly in finding good sales people and finding the right people for the right role. Cash flow: in how fast the money goes. This is the first startup I didn't bootstrap.

Q: What aspects of ownership are the most rewarding?

A: The sense of accomplishment. The relationships I've built,

HOLONYX

and having the ability to mentor others and share what I've learned.

Q: Are there one or two things you can attribute your success to? Luck, timing, someone who helped you?

A: Relationships are vitally important. Maintaining a can do attitude, in that you will always find a way, no matter what. Brent Bachman from Advanced Energy was one of my early role models.

Q: What is the most important attribute you look for in an employee?

A: I believe that you have to get the employees to drink the kool-aid, in that they have to really believe in the company and its products. Look to hire a diverse mix in

> *"You cannot motivate another person, all you can do is exploit what they are internally motivated by."*

thinking skills, specifically in problem solving skills. I look to create a team that fosters creative tension, in that the diversity of the team, with a shared desire for common good forces people to think differently. You cannot motivate another person, all you can do is exploit what they are internally motivated by. Good leaders and managers find a way to appeal to whatever motivates that person.

Q: Do you recommend any books, classes or websites? Do you recommend an MBA?

A: I do recommend an MBA, reason being that it gives you a structure to solve tough problems, but experience is equally important to learn how to think. Recommended reading: *Confessions of a Venture Capitalist* by Ruthann Quindlen and *Notes to Myself* by Hugh Prather.

Q: Slogan to live by or what it might say on your tombstone?

A: "Every human being desires to work under a ceiling of authority," – whether for an employer or a higher source. "He caused me to become," and also "You haven't heard the last of me."

RICH KOPCHO

Q: Anything else you want to add?

A: No matter where you work, ask the question "Is the head-ship going in the right direction? Do I trust in the head, and am I on board?" If not, start working in a new direction.

HOLONYX

"Make money and have fun."
David Lamb, Good Day Pharmacy

◆

BACKGROUND

David Lamb established Good Day Pharmacy in 1986 and today has 11 stores with over 90 employees. Good Day is David's 7th company, and he still owns or has previously owned a John Deere dealership, a consulting business, an Ice Rink, an outpatient surgery, and a mail order pharmacy.

INTERVIEW

Q: What was your initial startup cost and source?

A: [Didn't disclose startup cost.] The source was from personal savings.

Q: How long until you reached a positive cash flow?

A: Immediately because I bought a pre-existing pharmacy. However any new pharmacy we open now typically takes two years on average to break even.

Q: Did you use a business plan?

A: Yes, although not perhaps in the formal sense.

Q: Have you had to morph your original business plan to meet the demands of the market?

A: Yes, I continually update my plan.

Q: What is the community you serve and the passion that it fills for you personally?

A: We simply serve markets that other pharmacies don't. For me the business is fun and I like the social aspects of my job.

Q: Where do you see yourself and your company in 10 years?

A: I would like to stay involved in the business in a small way (perhaps a 10% stake), but for the most part be retired.

Q: Looking back now, is there anything you wish you had done differently?

A: I would have spent more time on gathering market analysis before selecting a location for a new pharmacy.

Q: What aspects of ownership are the most rewarding?

A: Being able to provide for my employees by giving them income and benefits. The financial rewards have been sweet and several more opportunities have arisen as a result of this business. Hard work has always been and continues to be rewarding.

> *"Honesty and integrity are vital for success, I've seen through the years that bad karma will eventually find you if you do someone wrong."*

Q: Are there one or two things you can attribute to your success? Luck, timing, someone who helped you?

A: Hard work and perseverance. My grandmother inspired me at a young age, she was an entrepreneur.

Q: How do you attract and retain the best employees? What is the most important attribute you look for?

A: I first look for people who have a strong personality. I believe in offering good employees the opportunity to move up, earn good pay, and provide a work-life balance by offering more flexibility than other pharmacies. I make a point to interview every pharmacist who expresses interest, whether or not we are hiring at the time.

> *"I would have spent more time on gathering market analysis..."*

Q: Do you recommend any books, classes or websites? Do you recommend an MBA?

A: Yes, I recommend an MBA for credibility and to learn the basics of running a business, especially to learn about the less

GOOD DAY PHARMACY

attractive parts like accounting. I listen to "Executive Book Summaries" and get ideas from them. I also subscribe to the "Trends-Future Club of America."

Q: Slogan to live by or what it might say on your tombstone?
A: "Make money and have fun", or "Someone's dysfunction is somebody else's opportunity."

Q: Anything else you would like to add?
A: I love competition and I'm a capitalist at heart. Honesty and integrity are vital for success, I've seen through the years that bad karma will eventually find you if you do someone wrong.

DAVID LAMB

"In the beginner's mind there are many possibilities, but in the expert's there are few."

- Shunryu Suzuki-Roshi, Soto Zen Priest

"Never give up."
Dan and Julie Lewis, Fossil Creek Gas Mart

◆

BACKGROUND
Dan and Julie Lewis purchased the Fossil Creek Gas Mart in 2006. They have two full time employees and after investing $125,000 in the business hope to be back in the black within 3 years. Prior to this business, they owned a drycleaners in Washington state that is now being run by their children.

INTERVIEW
Q: Did you use a business plan?
A: Yes.

Q: Have you had to change it to meet the needs of the market?
A: Yes, several times.

Q: The genesis of the idea?
A: Years ago, Dan was fired from his job, and he vowed he would never again work for someone else. He took every penny he had and bought the dry cleaning business in Washington. We have a partnership in a horse ranch up in Wyoming and we were spending more and more time in Fort Collins. We always knew we wanted to retire here. Since our kids were doing a fine job of running the family dry cleaning business in Washington, we felt like the time was right to make the move. The idea was to get to Fort Collins sooner than later, work a few more years and then retire. It did shock our kids, with the leap of faith we took.

Q: The vision of the company and the community you serve?
A: A warm and inviting community supported gas station that has other attractions as well, a place that people will want to

131

stop by to say hello and run into friends. We provide a level of service that far exceeds what people are used to getting when they stop in to refuel. Also, we are in the process of converting the car wash in the back into a drive-thru coffee shop.

Q: Where do you see yourself and your company in 10 years?

A: Not here. Hopefully retired and we will have sold the business.

Q: What have been your biggest challenges? Looking back now, is there anything you wish you had done differently?

A: We probably would have not purchased this particular business. This was the first business we bought, and we should have taken a closer look at the profit and loss papers, not blindly trusting what was provided to us. We wish we had done more market research on the area. While the highway out front has high traffic, people driving by tend to be more focused on a destination as they speed past. The city is now requiring all the businesses along this stretch to lower our signage, which will make us even less noticeable. When gas prices are high, the margins on the sale of gas alone don't pay the bills. We have a hard time competing with both the corporate owned stations (like BP, Shell, 7-11, etc.), as well as the larger retailers (like Costco, Safeway, etc.).

> *"You need to have a faith that things will work out, and whatever comes up, you can deal with."*

Q: Biggest rewards? What aspects of ownership are the most rewarding?

A: Having the ability to give our kids not only the business knowledge at a young age, but a business they can run themselves. It's rewarding to see them 100% self sufficient now. Showing them that you don't have to work for someone else.

Q: Are there one or two things you can attribute your success to? Luck, timing, someone who helped you?

A: Persistence and faith. Never quit. You need to have a faith that things will work out, and whatever comes up, you can

FOSSIL CREEK GAS MART

deal with. You have to get past your fears and I know it holds a lot of people back in life. We don't dwell on the setbacks, as we've had more than our share with this business. At times like these, we are grateful that we've survived another day.

Q: What is the most important attribute you look for in an employee?

A: Employee theft and turnover is a big problem. There is a lot of responsibility in this job with lottery tickets, cigarettes, and gas. Finding honest people has been tough, which is why we find ourselves working here far more than we expected.

Q: Do you recommend any books, classes or websites? Do you recommend an MBA?

A: No on the MBA. Experience is the best teacher, the school of hard knocks. Get involved with the community. We've contacted the local youth teams and allow them to have car washes here for fund raisers, it's a win-win because it also helps increase traffic to our store.

Q: Slogan to live by or what it might say on your tombstone?

A: "Never give up."

Q: Anything else you would like to add?

A: We see how many people are out of work right now because we see them put only $5 worth of gas in their car. It makes us grateful for what we do have, and with this perspective, we work a little harder for ourselves. There are a lot of sleepless nights and hard work involved with running your own business.

DAN AND JULIE LEWIS

"When a thing is new people say it is not true. Later when it's truth becomes obvious, they say it is not important. Finally, when it's importance cannot be denied, anyway, it is not new."

- William James

28

"He didn't know he couldn't fly, so he did."
Joseph Livengood, Livengood Engineering, Inc.

◆

BACKGROUND

Joseph Livengood, MD and Amy Livengood, BSN, RN are the founders of Livengood Engineering, Inc. The company located in Fort Collins, Colorado was established in 2004. They are in the medical device and equipment design and manufacturing industry and employee eight people. Dr. Livengood set up and managed a five-surgeon medical practice for two-and-a-half years.

INTERVIEW

Q: What was your initial startup cost and source of funding?
A: $200,000 from family, friends and myself.

Q: How long until there was a positive cash flow?
A: We are projecting four-and-a half to five years.

Q: Did you use a business plan?
A: Yes.

Q: Have you had to morph your original business plan to meet the demands of the market?
A: The business plan has been a point of exasperation and a focusing tool. It's not so much that we followed it but it made us commit our ideas to hardcopy and forced us to test theories that would otherwise potentially have been lost. It is a working document that becomes better as we learn about the market. Unfortunately, over a four-year period, the market has changed as well.

Q: What was the genesis of the idea?
A: Frustration because patients are tethered to their beds by

135

devices and cords attached to them when easily 85 percent of them should be walking. We took everything that may be attached or closely associated with the patient and determined how to bring these together onto a patient-manageable mobile structure. This led to the concept of the Livengood Platform that we expect will set a new standard for patient care.

Q: What came first, the problem or the solution?

A: The problem was certainly first. My wife has been a nurse and I am a general and trauma surgeon. The initial idea was how to free-up patients from the cables and devices that trap them in bed.

Q: What is the passion that it fills for you personally?

A: Contributing to the advancement of healthcare regarding the personal experience of both the patients and staff. It also fills my passion for design and problem solving. The challenge of having issues to address that span engineering, medicine and all aspects of business makes for never a dull moment.

Q: Where do you see yourself and your company in 10 years?

A: I would love to see our company become a strong R&D (Research and Development) company that continues to develop products related to the concepts that the platform enables. As R&D is spun out by the larger companies, I also see an opportunity to provide R&D both as a contracted service and as a company that spins out products to companies with focused distribution capabilities.

> *"Learning business is akin to saying you are learning medicine. The subject area is beyond huge. You can't possibly tackle all of it and you don't need to."*

Q: What were your biggest challenges? What do you know now that you wish you'd known sooner?

A: Finding the right people that are entrepreneurially-minded to help with the effort. Maintaining enough funding so that I can focus on moving forward rather than being in a constant

LIVENGOOD ENGINEERING, INC.

fund-raising effort. I wish I had done many things differently but I'm not sure how I could have known it was

> **"Don't spend a lot of money listening to self-proclaimed experts."**

wrong at the time. I wasted a lot of time and money chasing all of the "organizations" that claim to offer assistance to small companies. They attract dreamers, job-seekers and opportunists. The true support and money is found through social networks outside of these organizations.

Q: What were your biggest rewards?

A: We have seen the promise of a product that meets all of our initial goals come to fruition. An unexpected reward is the closeness that the group has developed to reach this goal.

Q: Are there one or two things you can attribute your success to?

A: They did a study to determine how to differentiate between an entrepreneur and a salesperson. The quality that stuck in my head is that an entrepreneur is one that sticks with a task long after any normal person would have, or should have stopped. That has been the quality that has kept us moving forward and on the verge of success.

Q: Was there one or two breakthroughs you can recall that really made the difference, and what led up them?

A: The biggest breakthrough was when we ran out of money while pursuing what we thought was our final design. It required over $600,000 in tooling to make one production model and no one was willing to take the risk. We had many great moments in design. This is when the team truly came together. Previous misconceptions were dumped, pride set aside and we redesigned the product from scratch. It was a very painful experience but truly the turning point that turned what would have been a disaster into the product we were looking for all along.

Q: How do you attract and retain the best employees? Your thoughts on the employee-ownership model?

A: It's personal. When you have a small company, times are bound to be tough and lean. Only those that feel a personal commitment to the cause of people will work through the challenges. Compensation is something that has to be individualized. Ownership offers a very delayed payback and may amount to nothing depending on future dilution, valuation and success.

> *"...an entrepreneur is one that sticks with a task long after any normal person would have, or should have stopped."*

Q: Do you recommend any books, classes or websites? Do you recommend an MBA?

A: Don't spend a lot of money listening to self-proclaimed experts. The true experts will come by referral and will offer their help without up-front fees. See what others are reading and keep the focus of your efforts on subjects that are either relevant or of some interest to you. Learning business is akin to saying you are learning medicine. The subject area is beyond huge. You can't possibly tackle all of it and you don't need to. MBAs are important for certain roles but don't get one unless you want one. Put yourself in the role that fits you, ignore the title, and surround yourself with the expertise that you lack. You are the leader and you have to be constantly learning everything you can to keep the show running and discover what it is that you don't know -- that you don't know. There is no "right" way to start a business, but I can probably give a better answer to what are the wrong things to do when starting a business.

Q: What is your slogan to live by or what it might say on your tombstone?

A: "He didn't know he couldn't fly, so he did."

LIVENGOOD ENGINEERING, INC.

"Live for yourself."
Rob McNealy, Contrived Media, Ltd.

◆

BACKGROUND

Rob McNealy founded Contrived Media Ltd., in Aurora, Colorado, in 2007. Contrived Media helps clients reach customers in venues outside normal corporate domains, such as social networking sites and other online communities. Their mission is to help companies build a positive online presence that both educates and persuades potential customers. Rob is perhaps best known as the host of *StartupStoryRadio.com* and *AskAFloorGuy.com*. He started two other companies prior to Contrived Media, and has been an entrepreneur for over 20 years.

INTERVIEW

Q: What was your initial startup cost and source?
A: $25k, bootstrapped (self-funded).

Q: How long until there was a positive cash flow?
A: 10 months.

Q: Did you use a business plan?
A: No.

Q: What is the vision of the company and the community you serve? What came first, the problem or the solution?
A: The problem always comes first. I look for needs in the market place and build solutions around those needs. Our content serves entrepreneurs, startups, and anyone seeking advice on flooring. My wife, Kristie, is a freelance author and medical blogger at *KristieMcNealy.com*.

Q: What is the passion that it fills for you personally?
A: I like to create, and the freedom and independence that

comes with doing what you love. It's a great feeling to have control over my life. My entrepreneurial roots can be traced back to the first commission-only job I took. During the job interview, while I pleaded my case for a salary, I was asked, "Why would you want to be limited by a paycheck?" It was only after I was running my own company that I realized the limits of being an employee working for a paycheck.

Q: What was the genesis of the idea?

A: I discovered that being an entrepreneur is actually more secure than being an employee, and I was driven to help others do the same. The genesis of our model came from many different places and continues to evolve. Early on I was intrigued by Tom Martino's *The Troubleshooter* model, where he was both a media personality and an entrepreneur.

Q: Where do you see yourself and your company in 10 years?

A: Semi-retired; having the option to choose whether or not I'll work, I know I will probably always work, as I like what I do.

Q: What have been the biggest rewards of ownership? Any unexpected rewards?

A: Having my wife as a business partner, and being able to spend more time with my family, which means more to me than anything else. It is mainly the intangibles that effort has produced. The sense of accomplishment that is proven by my success in business is a huge reward in my mind. Risk itself has a huge payoff. When Guy Kawasawki (*Art of the Start*) recommended my website on *Alltop.com*, I realized I had "made it." Guy is someone I admire, and to be recognized like that by someone you admire is success. Startup Story Radio has produced immense fulfillment, and opened doors that I would have never otherwise had. Unexpected rewards have been getting free tickets to events, books, and other merchandise from "my fans" who listen.

> *"It was only after I was running my own company that I realized the limits of being an employee working for a paycheck."*

Contrived Media, Ltd.

Q: Are there one or two things you can attribute your success to? Was it luck, timing, someone who helped you?

A: I believe in fate. Fate manifests itself through a series of "right time" opportunities aligning with luck. I know the harder I work, the luckier I am. I have learned that the more I help others become successful, the more successful I become myself. I've learned a recipe for success is in being able to recognize opportunities. As they all share certain key attributes, my ability to recognize those attributes has been the secret to my success.

> *"I don't look back and see any failures, only lessons learned."*

Q: What were your biggest challenges?

A: People. Specifically, I was crossed twice by partners. People problems kill companies. Cash flow was more of a challenge early on. Impatience is my greatest weakness. I don't look back and see any failures, only lessons learned. I think this is a common trait among entrepreneurs. My current businesses have been successful. Failure was never an option, so I didn't dwell on it.

Q: How do you attract and retain the best employees? What is the most important attribute you look for?

A: Number one, look for honesty. I spend a lot of time networking. I leverage the power of referrals. Someday I will write a book on networking.

Q: Any recommended training and resources? Books, classes, websites? Do you recommend an MBA?

A: Here's some valuable insight on the MBA path; if you intend to sell to big corporations, I recommend an MBA. I would add that if you plan to spend a lot of effort raising venture capital funding, then get an MBA as you will better understand the people you are selling to. The decision makers in large corporations and venture capitalists all commonly have MBA's. For books, I recommend *The Illusion of Entrepreneurship* by Scott A. Shane; *Art of the Start* by Guy Kawasaki; *The Virtues of Selfishness* by Ayn Rand and Nathaniel Branden; and *Rich*

ROB MCNEALY

Dad, Poor Dad by Robert T. Kiyosaki and Sharon L. Lechter, which addresses the psychology of fear. I highly recommend being a force in the blogsphere, and everything related to social networking: Facebook, Myspace, Twitter, Linkedin, etc. I suggest you develop a "Twitter" following! Brand yourself. Spend time getting your name out there and get recognized as "an expert." It's how you build your personal brand. I've done it with Startup Story Radio and Ask a Floor Guy. I also run several meetups, and helped launch the first ever *Thin Air Summit*.

Q: Slogan to live by or what it might say on your tombstone?
A: "Live for yourself."

Q: Anything else you would like to share?
A: I actually consider myself an "accidental entrepreneur." I did it for the lifestyle. Corporate healthcare is a conspiracy. There was a general consensus among a group of entrepreneurs in a venture capitalists forum I attended, where healthcare costs were seen as a barrier to entrepreneurship. The idea was that people who could be entrepreneurs are not willing to leave their corporate jobs because of the high cost of health insurance once you leave the company. This is false because there is cheap healthcare available for the self-employed, the big companies just don't want you to believe it exists.

CONTRIVED MEDIA, LTD.

ROB'S TIPS FROM THE TRENCHES

1. The way in which people speak separates entrepreneurs from employees.

2. Employees are dependent, entrepreneurs are interdependent.

3. Find a niche and go for it.

4. Get involved with TiE (The Indus Entrepreneurs). It's the largest non-profit for entrepreneurs and one of the best organizations I've found.

"Live Life to the Fullest."
Braun Mincher, Braun Media

◆

BACKGROUND
Braun Mincher is a young and successful entrepreneur who was able to "retire" at the age of 30. Braun is a self-made multi-millionaire even though he started with nothing and dropped out of college. Braun has started multiple companies. At 16, Braun started his first business and sold it two years later. Other start-ups include CTI Communications, LLC, Western Starr Charters and *TeamCellular.com* (visit *www.braunmincher.com* for a full list). He has recently undertaken a nationwide initiative to bring a new awareness of the "Financial Illiteracy Epidemic," and is traveling the country to further this important cause. Braun is a recognized expert in the field of personal finance who is frequently interviewed by the media. His credentials include being both a Licensed Real Estate Broker and a Licensed Mortgage Broker. Braun is challenging high schools and colleges across the nation to make Personal Finance classes a graduation requirement, just like math, English and science. Braun is the creator of *FinancialLiteracyQuiz.com*, and also the award-winning author of a new book, *The Secrets of Money: A Guide for Everyone on Practical Financial Literacy*. In addition to being a successful entrepreneur and author, Braun is also an experienced professional speaker who inspires, educates and entertains audiences of all sizes on the topics of leadership, entrepreneurship, business, and of course, personal finance.

INTERVIEW
Q: What was your initial startup cost and source?
A: In the case of Western Starr Charters, it was started with $7,500 from angel investors.

Q: How long until there was a positive cash flow?
A: 18 months.

Q: Did you use a business plan? Have you had to morph your original business plan to meet the demands of the market?

A: Yes. The business model was expanded to capture new opportunities and fulfill areas of demand.

Q: The vision of the company and the community you serve? What came first, the problem or the solution?

A: I learned a simple system for financial success, and now I pursue my passion of better educating all consumers (regardless of age, income or education level), not just the business or financial savvy, on the topic of "Practical Financial Literacy." This is done with the philosophy that Financial Literacy = Financial Success. I have spent the last 12 months traveling nationwide raising awareness of what I see as the "Financial Illiteracy Epidemic."

> *"To sum up my 'keys to success', I would say you must be willing to take risks and work hard."*

Q: What is the passion that it fills for you personally?

A: Both independence and autonomy. I truly enjoy hard work.

Q: What was the genesis of the idea?

A: In the case of Western Starr Charters, I saw a better way to do it. I actually took my business plan to my old boss and he wouldn't even consider it. The bottom line was, I felt he could do it better and I was right.

Q: Where do you see yourself and your company in 10 years?

A: I am not sure, but I will always be open to new things. I see the businesses I currently own as being expanded or sold.

Q: What were your biggest challenges? What do you know now that you wish you'd known sooner?

A: Raising capital would be the biggest challenge. I learned it was necessary to find good employees – people who share my passion and vision.

Q: What have been the biggest rewards? Any unexpected rewards?

A: The recognition (I was interviewed on the TODAY show), the financial rewards and being in control. I admit that I am a control freak.

Q: Are there one or two things you can attribute your success to? Was it luck, timing, someone who helped you, etc.?

A: My parents inspired me at a young age, which I talk about in my book. I also get inspiration and ideas from business magazines. The DECA program in high school helped me to write my first business plan. In my bus transportation business, there was one large contract we won that was largely responsible for sustaining the growth of the company. To sum up my "keys to success", I would say you must be willing to take risks and work hard, but for a more expanded answer to this question, read chapter 10 of my book *The Secrets of Money*.

> *"...if you get a client based on price, you will lose that client based on price."*

Q: What is the most important attribute you look for? Any thoughts on the employee-ownership model?

A: The most important thing is to find people who are passionate. They should show up to work for more than just the paycheck. If someone comes on board because of the paycheck, they will leave for the same reason. Similarly, if you get a client based on price, you will lose that client based on price. Yes, I am indeed a fan of the employee ownership model.

Q: Do you recommend any books, classes or web sites? Do you recommend an MBA?

A: I admit that I don't read too many books, but I do spend a fair amount of time reading trade journals and early in my career, business magazines like Inc., Entrepreneur, Success, and so on. I don't have an MBA. I didn't finish college, so I can't comment on whether or not I'd recommend it, but I definitely see the value in learning. Although I firmly believe that experience is the best teacher.

BRAUN MINCHER

Q: What is your slogan to live by or what it might say on your tombstone?

A: "Live life to the fullest."

Braun Media

31

"Follow your passion and everything else will work out."

Jim Mofhitz, Humorous Clocks

◆

BACKGROUND

Jim Mofhitz, of Wellington, Colorado, established Humorous Clocks, his first true venture in the arts and crafts industry, in 1981. When he noticed his part-time hobby as a clock maker was earning more than his job as a controller for Glen Glenn Sound, he decided to go for it full time. During the craft show season, Jim works twelve hours a day, seven days a week; but he said it never feels like work because this was a hobby before, and it still feels like a hobby. He thinks that statement shows a critical common element among successful entrepreneurs: they work long hours, but the hours rarely feel like work because when you are doing something you are passionate about, something that fulfills a deep purpose within you, you'll be at it for hours upon hours, and it'll feel effortless. Jim has two employees, and used to pay $100 a design to a professional calligrapher and printer for the clock faces he designed. Today he uses Corel Draw, and you can't tell the difference between what was done by a calligrapher, and what was done by the computer. He admits initially there was a lot of resistance to moving over to the computer because it was "uncomfortable," but today he can create any customized clock face for virtually no cost because of it. Jim feels lucky that he's found a way to turn his hobby into a way to pay the bills.

INTERVIEW

Q: What was your initial startup cost and source?
A: $1,200, savings.

Q: How long until there was a positive cash flow?
A: Immediate.

Q: Did you use a business plan?

A: Not a formal one, but I do have to plan out which craft shows I want to participate in each year because you have to submit your applications early, and I also need to build up enough inventory.

Q: What is the vision of the company and the community you serve? Which came first, the problem or the solution?

A: I love woodworking. The detail and quality of clocks is appreciated, and I have pride in what I build. The humorous clocks used to represent only a small part of what I took to craft shows, but turned out to be my biggest seller. Today I have over 250 different clocks, and commonly do custom orders allowing my clients to have a unique one-of-a-kind clock.

> *"I made more in two days than I did in a month as a controller."*

Q: What is the passion that it fills for you personally?

A: I love going to the craft shows and meeting so many interesting people. The appreciation I receive from others who enjoy my product is rewarding.

Q: What was the genesis of the idea?

A: I was making clocks as a hobby when people started asking me to make clocks for them. When I noticed my part-time hobby as a clock maker was earning more than my job as a controller, I decided to go for it full time. In one of my first craft shows, "Gilroy Garlic Festival", I made more in two days than I did in a month as a controller.

> *"My background as an accountant has helped me stay in business by staying focused on the numbers."*

Q: Where do you see yourself and your company in 10 years?

A: Retired. Not sure if the business will be viable enough to sell or not, but I would like to see someone who is as passionate about the craft as I am to continue making the product.

HUMOROUS CLOCKS

Q: What were your biggest challenges?

A: Traveling as much as 229 days a year, and having left over inventory.

Q: What have been your biggest rewards?

A: The appreciation I get directly from my customers. Doing what I love, and having an outlet for my creativity.

Q: Are there one or two things you can attribute your success to?

A: My background as an accountant has helped me stay in business by staying focused on the numbers. You need to be careful not to over-spend, and be realistic on the profits. I use a spreadsheet (see sample on next page) that highlights the most important indicators of whether or not a show I did made any money or not.

> *"Too many people in the craft business get buried because they lack common business sense."*

Q: Any recommended training and resources? Books, classes, websites? Do you recommend an MBA?

A: No on the MBA, but you do need to understand how business works. Too many people in the craft business get buried because they lack common business sense. For resources a couple of great sites are *FNO.com* and *craftreporter.com*.

Q: Slogan to live by or what It might say on your tombstone?

A: "Follow your passion and everything else will work out," and "He tried and tried, and finally died."

Q: Are there any areas where you need help?

A: Online marketing. Today, my website represents only seven percent of my sales. If I could get this number up, I would be able to travel fewer days a year.

JIM MOFHITZ

Q: Anything else?

A: I am always surprised at the number of people who work craft shows but have never looked back to see if it was profitable. I keep track of every show I have a booth at using a spreadsheet. Some are worth my time, others are not. Occasionally, I've even taken a loss. It helps me decide which shows to attend each year and which ones to pass up. Here's the simple profit/loss worksheet I use:

HUMOROUS CLOCKS

Date	March 1st, 2008
Show name	SF Craft Fair
Total Sales	**$3,000**
Cost of Goods Sold	-$450
Auto Mileage (x.52/mi.)	-$182
Lodging ($60/day)	-$120
Show Fees	-$300
Other Expenses (# of clocks sold x $6)	-$300
Total Expenses	**-$1352**
Net Profit	**$1648**

32

"She chooses happiness."
Jen, The Millionaire Mommy Next Door

◆

BACKGROUND

Jen grew up in a family where money was a constant source of tension and stress. Despite being intelligent, well-educated and hard-working, her parents lived paycheck to paycheck. This motivated Jen to break the cycle and learn about personal finance and as a result, she created a lifetime financial plan that enabled her to be free of money worries by age 40. In the process, Jen owned a dog training school and a co-owned a plumbing business. Currently, she shares her recipe for success, happiness and financial freedom on her blog which you can visit at *MillionaireMommyNextDoor.com*, and offers personalized life coaching and workshops. She is also writing a book.

INTERVIEW

Q: What was your initial startup cost and source?

A: Zero. I started with a free domain for my blog and avoided advertising expenses by creating "blogosphere buzz" online by word of mouth.

Q: How long until you had reached a positive cash flow?

A: Immediate. I enrolled in an Amazon Affiliates program to earn commissions from relevant book sales. I started out earning pennies. But once my blog traffic grew, I was able to enroll in an advertising network to make money based on the number of eyeballs that viewed my page. But I don't keep my blogging revenue. As part of my commitment to community, I pledge my blogging revenue as 0% microloans, through *Kiva.org*, to small businesses operated by working, impoverished women in developing countries.

Q: Did you use a business plan?

151

A: I researched the art and monetization of blogging, determined my niche and explored my target audience. I networked both online and offline, and I joined a writing critique group to develop my writing style.

Q: The genesis of the idea?

A: As a new mom eager for adult companionship, I sought a community of like-minded, creative women. I was introduced to a local writers group. My new friends believed that I had a story to tell, and I was encouraged to share it. I am an avid reader of blogs, and I really like that style of communication. Once my blog caught on, readers requested coaching and literary agents asked if I'd like to write a book. The business seems to be growing organically.

> "I discovered that once I chose happiness, the money followed."

Q: The vision of the company and the community you serve?

A: I serve the average everyday Jane seeking easy to understand financial education. I also write on topics regarding lifestyle design, proactive gratitude, happiness, and achieving one's personally defined measure of success. I discovered that once I chose happiness, the money followed. My top priorities are to enjoy life, spend time with my family, and never work overtime. This will always remain a part-time business.

Q: What is the passion that it fills for you personally?

A: I love to share what I've learned with others. Blogging is a creativity outlet and it allows me to express myself, hit the publish button and get immediate feedback from my readers. With individualized coaching, I can focus on results and help within a supportive and confidential one-on-one relationship.

Q: Where do you see yourself and your company in 10 years?

A: I can do this from anywhere in the world, and since I love to travel, I see my family and I exploring the world, empowering other people through financial education so they too can enjoy the life they want to live. I'm keeping an open mind as new opportunities present themselves and striving to maintain a healthy work – life balance.

Q: Biggest challenges? Looking back now, is there anything you wish you had done differently?

A: I started blogging in July 2007 on a free domain (blogspot). My readership grew quickly and soon all of my blog's link backs were attached to the blogspot domain. Then in October of 2008, the unthinkable happened. My entire Google account was disabled. This means my blog, my email account, my calendar, the whole shebang – were gone. I filled out all of the forms and all I got back from Google was this automated message, "Thank you for your report. The account in question is disabled, and we can't provide you with access to it." I have no idea why. I hadn't violated any of the terms of agreements, so I'm guessing that someone hacked into my account. Consequently, I secured my own URL and hosting services and started my blog all over again. If you are serious about blogging, do it on your own URL.

Q: Biggest rewards?

A: Freedom. Following my own rule book. Paying it forward and helping other people.

Q: Are there one or two things you can attribute your success to? Luck, timing, someone who helped you?

A: I create treasure maps that help me visualize the life I want to lead. I paste magazine pictures and words onto a poster board, then hang it on the wall over my computer and update it as necessary. I've learned that if you don't like the story your life has become, tell yourself a better one. The more comfortable you feel with the life you've visualized, the more your thoughts direct your actions. And of course when your actions change, your life circumstances change. I created my first "Treasure Map to a Rich Life" in my early twenties. A few years later, I was living the story

> *"I've learned that if you don't like the story your life has become, tell yourself a better one."*

I had envisioned through the treasure map tacked upon my wall. Every few years, life experiences modify some of my

JEN

aspirations and passions and my vision of wealth and happiness change, so I design a new treasure map. Lo and behold, my life soon morphs to fit my new vision. And it repeats over and over again.

Q: How do you attract and retain the best employees? The most important attribute?

A: Find others who share your passion for the vision of your business. I look for individuals that demonstrate integrity, honesty, and good people skills.

Q: Can you recommend any training or resources such as books, classes, or websites? Do you recommend an MBA?

A: I was a college drop out. I was an excellent student, but I decided that a college degree wasn't necessary to ensure my future success. I found faster, more efficient ways to start making money. I sought mentors and became an apprentice instead. The resources page on my blog lists the websites and books I recommend (visit *millionairemommynextdoor. com/resources)*. My favorite books include *Your Money or your Life, The Millionaire Next Door: The Surprising Secrets of America's Wealthy* by Thomas J. Stanley, and two great books by Barbara Sher: *WishCraft* and *I Could Do Anything If I Only Knew What It Was: How to Discover What You Really Want and How to Get It.*

Q: Slogan to live by or what it might say on your tombstone?

A: "She chooses happiness."

Q: Anything else?

A: Give before you ask for something in return. In one of my prior businesses, I offered free workshops. From the workshops, business was then referred to me so I never had to spend a dime on advertising.

"When you leave this world, strive to leave the world just a little bit better than when you arrived."
Ken Munsch, Cattleman's Choice Loomix

◆

BACKGROUND
Ken Munsch started working for Loomix in 1978, which was later sold to P.M. Ag Products in 1991. He worked his way up to become General Manager of the company's liquid feed division. Ken Munsch and his partner, Mike Troska, established Cattleman's Choice Loomix in 1997 after having the opportunity to spin off the division Ken was running at Loomix. Cattleman's Choice Loomix has approximately 350 distributors. They have enjoyed 10% plus annual growth since 1997 and are eight times larger today than at inception. Ken wasn't always his own boss. In his youth, he worked at a 24-hour gas station and worked 24-hour shifts!

INTERVIEW
Q: What was the genesis of the idea?
A: There was something we call "the three bucket test" that actually served as the delivery system for the liquid feed. The "three bucket test" was where three buckets of feed would be offered up to livestock to see which they prefer. It was during one such test that we stumbled upon a proprietary blend that made all the difference and it became a key product that helped fuel Loomix's growth ever since.

Q: What was your initial startup cost and source?
A: $500,000 from angel investors and $500,000 from banks.

Q: How long until you saw a positive cash flow?
A: It was immediate. Our company was profitable and cash-flowed from day one. As the company grew much larger we experienced cash-flow issues due to rapid growth. We were fortunate that our asset base also grew very rapidly and we

155

were able to cash-flow with our assets.

Q: Did you use a business plan?

A: Yes, I did. In fact, my partner Mike and I locked ourselves away in a hotel for three days while we wrote the business plan. In fact, every year, our management team has a retreat where we create a detailed strategic plan.

Q: What is the vision of the company and the community you serve?

A: Our company's roots date back to 1952. Our primary business is supplying vitamins and minerals to momma cows. We are like the GNC to momma cows. We also have a secondary company that imports European Technology to the United States primarily to be used by high-performance animals. In Europe you cannot use drugs on animals without a prescription. Of course in America, we can use a lot of drugs over the counter. For example, we market our product to the thoroughbred industry. In that one industry alone, we have 23 of the top 40 thoroughbred trainers using our product. We market our products through distributors, dealers, and through the internet.

> *"...Mike and I locked ourselves away in a hotel for three days while we wrote the business plan. "*

Q: What is the passion that it fills for you personally?

A: Creating a legacy of being the best in our industry. I have a real passion for the company, as does my wife. When I say company I mean our entire *Loomix* family encompassing our entire staff, dealers and their families.

Q: Where do you see yourself and your company in 10 years?

A: I see myself either working on very large expansion projects or more in a consulting position. As a company we have in place early parts of a succession strategy for key management. I see our company doubling in size within 10 years.

Q: Looking back now, is there anything you wish you had done differently? What do you know now that you wish you'd known sooner?

A: I would have hired different people with different skill sets sooner. Don't be afraid to hire people smarter than you, and don't hire people like you. Bring in people with strengths where you are weak. Give away less in the beginning.

Q: What were some of your biggest challenges?

A: We underestimated our value. Cash flow was a biggie. You have to manage growth and not grow too fast.

Q: What aspects of ownership are the most rewarding?

A: Being able to control where the money goes. It's very fulfilling to be the one making a difference in so many people's lives.

Q: Are there one or two things you can attribute your success to? Luck, timing, someone who helped you?

A: Luck and timing definitely helped, but patience was key. Integrity is everything. Three things in my life come before all else: my faith, my family, and my job. Also, I try to live by the saying: "Control the market data, and you'll control the market." That is something I learned in *The Ultimate Sales Machine* by Chet Holmes. Embracing my competition has helped, as well as being active with trade organizations.

> *"Three things in my life come before all else: my faith, my family, and my job."*

Q: How do you attract and retain the best employees, and in your case, dealers as well?

A: I am a big proponent of employee ownership. Ownership can mean getting a part of the bottom-line or having full accountability to your job. Full accountability means making the decisions and getting credit for the results. I still personally interview all candidates and we believe in a multi level interviewing strategy. We do the same when recruiting dealers. We interview them and check them out. We reward our top performers when we induct them into our '1000-ton Club' or another level of achievement at our 'Awards Ban-

KEN MUNSCH

quet'. I treat every employee and many of the dealers as if he or she were a part of my own immediate family and I pay attention to what's happening in his or her life. Every year, I spend a day with a sales rep in the field and I learn a great deal of valuable insights that I have always taken back to our senior management team.

Q: Do you recommend an MBA?

A: Yes! I would highly recommend an MBA. It is important for any path in life. I believe the MBA's we have on staff received real practical application of business life during the period they received their MBA education.

Q: What about recommendations for useful books?

A: *Good to Great* by Jim Collins, and *Ultimate Sales Machine* by Chet Holmes. Chet's book teaches something I experienced first hand. The only sales call I ever took was from a company who had uncovered the 'top 10 reasons feed businesses fail'. I was interested and learned that one of the 10 reasons was poor advertising, which was what the company who wrote the report was selling. Genius!

> *"Every year, I spend a day with a sales rep in the field and learn a great deal of valuable insights..."*

Q: What is a slogan to live by or what it might say on your tombstone?

A: That is an easy one because I have told many, many, people this throughout the years. I hope my tombstone says, "When you leave this world, strive to leave the world just a little bit better than when you arrived." And I hope there is an asterisk saying, "He did".

Q: Anything else you would like to share?

A: When we started Cattleman's Choice Loomix I knew that we needed to have about $1M to get started. I remember the old story Zig Ziglar used to tell about selling the "difference" not the whole picture. He tells a great story about his wife wanting to purchase a home in the Dallas market that was out of their price range. I don't remember the numbers but their price range was say $250K at that time in their life. His wife found a home that was $325K that she wanted to purchase. In Zig's books, and his speeches, he always tells someone when faced with that situation to sell the "difference" not the full value.

It was already a given that Zig would pay $250K; so his wife learning from Zig's preaching, knew that she only had to sell him on $75K. She got Zig to agree that $325K was not the issue but rather $75K.

When Zig grew up, he hung around some friends that were country club members and they could access the country club swimming pool any time they chose. Zig was not as fortunate and could only go to the pool as a guest of his friends. It seems one time he went without his friends and got caught and they threw him out. The country club had a unique styled swimming pool and Zig swore that day, someday he would have a pool like that at his home. Zig's wife took Zig on a tour of the $325K home getting him to agree that it was a nice home but still out of their price range. At the end of the tour she showed him the pool in the backyard that was identical to the pool Zig used to swim at when he grew up at the country club. His wife asked the question, "Is this pool worth $75K?" Zig rapidly agreed and he was sold on the difference and in reality he was sold on $325K.

Zig told that story at our National Dealer Meeting in Arroyo Grande, California. I am sure that I have some of the facts a little off but I have never forgotten that story and I have never forgotten to "sell the difference". Mike and I were cash poor when we started Cattleman's Choice Loomix but we knew that we needed $1M. I felt that if I could raise $500K, then I could raise the other $500K. So I focused on the difference of raising $500K, not $1M. It seemed like such a smaller hurdle to jump. In a matter of weeks we raised $500K without giving up any personal guarantees, only a small percentage of the business. With that $500K, I went to a bank with a good business plan and walked out with another $500K. We now had our $1M! With the first million in the bank it was a lot easier to multiply it into additional millions down the road. So what I would do with $20K is turn it first into $40K, and build it into a million.

KEN'S TIPS FROM THE TRENCHES

1. Hire different people, with a different set of skills.
2. Embrace your competition.
3. Get your MBA!
4. Leave the world better than when you arrived.

Author's Note:
Be sure to check out Ken's essay, *Appendix A:*
A Life Driven By Values. In it, he highlights the ten values that he lives by and the importance of finding good mentors along the way.

"Whatever you give out, you get back."
Larry Nelson, w3w3®

◆

BACKGROUND
Larry Nelson founded the Institute for Change Research International in 1993 and is the cofounder of w3w3® Talk Radio. Larry started over a dozen companies in six countries over the past three decades. He is a published author, trainer, keynote speaker, and most notably a business development architect. Larry is the author of *Mastering Change: Challenges, Choices and Champions* and coauthor of *Colorful Leadership*.

INTERVIEW
Q: What was your initial startup cost and source of funding?
A: Nothing.

Q: How long until there was a positive cash flow?
A: Immediately.

Q: Did you use a business plan?
A: No

Q: What was the genesis of the idea?
A: I was good at making millions of dollars and losing millions of dollars. This prompted my quest to find out why. I spent years researching my own strengths and weaknesses to uncover why my mind was already made up before I began. What I learned was to rejoice in everything I've got, especially my failures!

Q: What is the vision of the company?
A: To link people and organizations to unique and valuable resources. The three key aspects I always strive for are powerful, proven, and people-oriented people.

Q: What is the passion that this fills for you personally?

A: Being able to make a difference and help people get what they really want, even if they don't know what that is yet.

Q: Where do you see yourself in 10 years?

A: I see myself as a bestselling author and speaker. I would like to spend more time with my kids and grandkids, and start a school for kids.

Q: What was your biggest challenge? What do you know now that you wish you had known sooner?

A: I found out you need to hire the right people. I didn't listen to my gut when it came to building a team. It is best to hire people in areas where you are weak and do your due diligence in checking them out. I learned from my mishaps. I've had employees and partners steal various amounts of money over the years totaling millions of dollars. Use your head and your gut.

> *"It is best to hire people in areas where you are weak..."*

Q: What has been your biggest reward?

A: Helping people get what they really want, and discovering what that might be. Be it money, love, or whatever!

Q: Are there one or two things you can attribute your success to? Was it luck, timing, or maybe someone who helped you?

A: When I was young, I was recruited by a coin collector to find rare pennies. What came to me, was that I could recruit others to help me look for them. I figured out early on, that I could keep a cut for every rare penny they found, which I would then bring back to the coin collector. I learned later on that this was the same method that Mark Twain used when he got others to paint fences for him. When I was 21, I received a $50,000 loan, from the Small Business Administration (SBA) and my bank, to open my own stamp/coin collector store.

Q: Do you recommend an MBA?

w3w3®

A: Yes, I would recommend an MBA, but be sure to pick a good program. While pursuing it, make sure you get a lot of real world exposure. That being said, I once ran into a buddy who had a master's degree, and guess what he was doing? He was pumping gas. Entrepreneurs need plenty of MBAs around them since they make great employees. I was a college drop-out. I regret not spending more time in school.

> *"...I would recommend an MBA, but be sure to pick a good program."*

Q: What books would you recommend for the prospective entrepreneur?

A: *Think and Grow Rich* by Napoleon Hill and *As a Man Thinketh* by James Allen.

Q: What is your slogan to live by or what might it say on your tombstone?

A: "Whatever you give out, you get back." This holds true for your thoughts as well as your words and actions.

LARRY NELSON

Author's Note:
Be sure to check out *Appendix D: Business Networking Tips* by Larry. It's a must read in any industry.
Networking is a key tool for the savvy entrepreneur. Done right, it is an inexpensive form of marketing and can lead to great exposure. Not to mention immense success!

"Knowing others is intelligence; knowing yourself is true wisdom. Mastering others is strength; mastering yourself is true power."

- Lao Tzu

35

"A good guy that made a positive impact on others."
Jeff Nuttall, Northern Colorado Business Report, Inc.

◆

BACKGROUND

In 1995, Jeff Nuttall founded the Northern Colorado Business Report, Inc. (NCBR) in Fort Collins with the help of Chris Wood, Jeff Schott, and Jerry Lewis. From humble beginnings, he has grown his company to over 40 employees and achieved success against five other competing publishing companies. NCBR utilizes an integrated marketing concept of print, online, and special events to provide business content and information to Loveland and Larimer County. He attributes his success to outworking everyone else and applying the SWOT (Strength, Weakness, Opportunities, and Threats) technique to every major project. He also owns a stake in Data Joe, a database company, which is a key differentiator for his business.

INTERVIEW

Q: What was your initial startup cost and source?
A: $250k from personal and partners' sources.

Q: How long until there was a positive cash flow?
A: Three years.

Q: Did you use a business plan?
A: Yes.

Q: Have you had to morph your original business plan to meet the demands of the market?
A: Yes, several times. A business plan should be an ongoing work in progress.

Q: What was the genesis of the idea?
A: I was bit by the entrepreneurial bug at a young age during

an experience as an activities coordinator for an apartment complex where I started a newsletter to serve a 950+ unit community. I began to sell ads in it to local retailers and things really started to take off. After 8 years with the *Denver Business Journal*, I made it known that I was leaving to start my own marketing company. Jerry Lewis, managing editor for the *Denver Business Journal* and *Boulder County Business Report*, approached me with the idea for NCBR since he and I balanced our skills out well. He was strong on editing and I was strong in marketing and sales. Chris Wood, a former journalism student at CU and intern for Jeff Schott also joined us. One of the big attractors for us was the opportunity to live in Fort Collins.

Q: What is the vision of the company and the community you serve?

A: We provide business news content and information to Larimer and Weld County. To our advertisers, we offer a powerful integrated marketing strategy. Effective advertising is about frequent touches to the right prospects, in a variety of ways (leveraging print, online, and special events). Our sister company, DataJoe LLC, has powerful databases that continue to be a key differentiator for us.

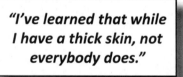

"I've learned that while I have a thick skin, not everybody does."

Q: What is the passion that it fills for you personally?

A: I've always enjoyed "being in the know," and having a pulse on what is going on, and I feel we are making a positive impact on the local business community.

Q: Where do you see yourself and your company in 10 years?

A: Leveraging new technology to parse out the news we receive. In the future, news is going to be customized to each of us based on our individual preferences. Whatever we are interested in, news we delivered through the means we chose. I also see NCBR moving to a more frequent weekly paper, delivering more events, and having a video room.

Q: What were your biggest challenges?

A: Human resources, people, have always been our biggest challenge. Bringing everyone together to produce a newspaper is no small task, to get everyone on 'the same page' when we all have such different perspectives. I believe that in any business, people can present the single biggest distraction. I've learned that while I have a thick skin, not everybody does. It's helped me to tone down my approach. It's all about being humble.

Q: What have been your biggest rewards? What aspects of ownership are the most rewarding?

A: Employee satisfaction, compliments from our clients, creating something from nothing, earning the respect of my peers, and high quality work/life balance. DataJoe LLC was definitely an unexpected success, it was never part of our original business plan. I got chance to bring one of my favorite authors, Joe Pine, to our *BIXPO* event in 2007.

Q: Are there one or two things you can attribute your success to? Was it luck, timing, or someone who helped you?

A: Luck, yes. But we were competing against five other papers when we started, and just outworked everyone else. SWOT (Strength, Weakness, Opportunities, Threats) every major project. Key to our success is an annual staff retreat where we define excellence goals. We then publish an internal dashboard every two weeks to track progress on the goals defined at the annual retreats.

> *"Key to our success is an annual staff retreat where we define excellence goals."*

Q: How do you attract and retain the best employees? What is the most important attribute you look for?

A: We give our people autonomy and include them in decision making. We have a weekly manager meetings where everyone is free to share whatever is on his/her mind. Synergies occur and problems get flushed out. We strive to hire entrepreneurial thinking people, make them managers, and include them in decision making.

Making sure we are hiring for what the job requires, and tapping into what motivates them to maximize creativity, energy, and entrepreneurial spirit. The right combination of energy and creativity is powerful. I'm a fan of the PDP (Professional Dynametric Program) to measure energy level and help identify if they have the right traits for the job. We also use it on an ongoing basis to help discover what motivates our employees. We have a great team, which is why the interviewing process is so important.

Q: Any recommended training and resources? Books, classes, Websites? Do you recommend an MBA?

A: *Good to Great* by Jim Collins; *Stomp the Elephant* by Steve Vannoy and Craig Ross; and *The Experience Economy and Authenticity*, by Joe Pine and James Gilmore. Yes on the MBA, and Denver University has a great entrepreneur program where they help you put together your own business plan. You walk away with what you need to launch your own business.

> *"How you stage things has everything in the world to do with how successful you are."*

Q: Slogan to live by or what it might say on your tombstone?

A: "A good guy that made a positive impact on others."

Q: Anything else you'd like to add?

A: I'm a big fan of the philosophy behind the book *The Experience Economy* by B. Joseph Pine and James H. Gilmore. It's the idea that business is a theater, and the playing field is a stage. How you stage things has everything in the world to do with how successful you are. Tom Livingston brought that book to our attention because he recognized how we bring the people and companies from our paper out into the real world. It's all about bringing people together, which for me has been the most rewarding.

36

"If you have a dream, take a chance on it!"
Doug Odell, Odell Brewing Company

◆

BACKGROUND
In 1989. Doug Odell established Odell Brewing Company (OBC), the first microbrewery in Fort Collins, Colorado. Today OBC employs 45 people and is one of the most respected companies in the area. Odell's beer is currently distributed in eight states: Arizona, Colorado, Wyoming, South Dakota, Nebraska, Kansas, Missouri and New Mexico. For a short time, Doug worked at Anchor Brewing in San Francisco back in the late 1970s where he had held one of the worst jobs in the brewery, cleaning out the mash tubs and brew kettles. And prior to OBC, Doug ran a landscaping business in Seattle. Doug was first active in the local homebrew club, but when he decided to open the brewery, a couple others took notice and opened their own breweries shortly thereafter (New Belgium and H.C. Berger). Fort Collins has since become one of the hottest spots in the country for microbrewers.

INTERVIEW
Q: What was your initial startup cost and source of funding?
A: $135,000 which was the proceeds from the sale of our home in Seattle and some angel funding from family and friends. About a year after we opened, we went back and bought out the investors.

Q: How long until there was a positive cash flow?
A: 18 months. My wife, Wynne, maintained a corporate job to cover my lack of a paycheck during those first 18 months.

Q: Did you use a business plan?
A: Yes, and looking back, it shows how ignorant we were at the time, but it was useful to provide direction and maintain fo-

169

cus.

Q: What was the genesis of the idea?

A: My wife and I had decided early on that we wanted to be self employed. Our thought was that we could either take the landscaping company I already had and build it up or we could take a closer look at a this new "craft brewing" movement that was beginning to form in the Pacific Northwest. I was already a home brewer and noticed the powerful impact these new microbreweries were having on people. Initially,

> *"...I should have handed over more responsibility to others sooner."*

we wanted to open a brewery in western Washington, but the area was already fairly saturated with breweries. We looked at Flagstaff, Arizona and Northern Colorado. My wife's sister lived in Northern Colorado and Fort Collins seemed to make the most sense.

Odell Brewing Company

Q: What is the vision of the company and the community you serve?

A: We've evolved to become a large contributor to our community; it's our way of giving back to the community that has given us so much. In fact, we've found that the more we give, the more we get back.

Q: What is the passion that it fills for you personally?

A: I'm passionate about beer! I like experimenting with different recipes and coming up with a finished product that people love. People are truly enthusiastic about good beer.

Q: Looking back now, is there anything you wish you had done differently?

A: The importance of delegating responsibility and doing it as soon as you can was a bit challenging. It's something that was very hard for me. For the first four years, I didn't take more than three business days off. In hindsight, I should have handed over more responsibility to others sooner.

Q: What is your biggest reward?

A: The positive recognition the brewery gets. Peer recognition when we win awards at the tasting competitions. Learning the entire end-to-end brewing process. Giving back to the community. The impressive reaction others get when they learn that you work for a brewery.

Q: Are there one or two things you can attribute your success to? Was it luck, timing, someone who helped you, etc?

A: Greg Bujak, a homebrew shop owner in Seattle, helped to convince me that I could start a brewery. I remember spend-ing hours with him at his shop talking about brew-ing. Shortly after I opened the brewery, I invited Greg out to Fort Collins and he brewed a few batches with

> *"We hire people who truly want to come to work here and do so for more than a paycheck."*

me. We didn't hire our first employee until May of 1990, and not having a salary to pay helped at the start when money was tight. I don't get very concerned about risk and have plenty of self-confidence in my abilities. We went through a significant shift about five years ago after we realized we had hit a plateau in our business. We hired a sales and marketing manager who knew what to do, and it has made a big differ-ence.

Q: How do you attract and retain the best employees? What is the most important attribute you look for? Do you have any thoughts on the employee-ownership model?

A: The best employees are eager to take on responsibility and take ownership of problems. They are always looking for ways to do things better and willing to lend a hand to fellow employees. One of the questions we ask in the interview is, "Why do you want to work at OBC?" and that answer usually tells us a lot. If they are just looking for another job, then they are not the right fit. We hire people who truly want to come to work here and do so for more than a paycheck. We don't offer a formal employee share plan, but three employ-ees do indeed have stock in the company.

Q: Where do you see yourself and your company in 10 years?

A: I plan to be retired and we are beginning to take a look at

DOUG ODELL

all our options. I think it is important for an entrepreneur to realize that at some point in a company's evolution, they need to take themselves out of the top position. I believe it's essential for the health and growth of the company. The success of the brewery has far exceeded what I ever imagined, although I never gave it much thought.

Q: Are there any books, classes or training you recommend? Do you recommend an MBA?

A: No on the MBA, at least in the beginning. Some knowledge of how to run a business is important. As a company grows, having someone with an MBA is very helpful. I took some fermentation classes at UC Davis, but I learned the most by talking to others involved in the many aspects of the brewing industry and just by doing it myself. I tend to read biographies, for example: *Beer School: Bottling Success at the Brooklyn Brewery* by the founders Steve Hindy and Tom Potter.

Q: What is your slogan to live by or what it might say on your tombstone?

A: "If you have a dream, take a chance on it". Dreams don't come true by thinking about them, you have to get out there and do it.

Q: Is there anything else that I didn't ask that would be wise advice to an aspiring entrepreneur?

A: Be patient. Don't get ahead of yourself. Be self-disciplined enough to do the things that need to get done, even if they aren't the things you want to do. I don't tend to think much about the long-term, but I realize that having a five-year plan is important and something we need to do. Also, it is important to recognize when you've reached the limit of your own ability and need to acquire new talent that can take you to the next level.

> *"...I learned the most by talking to others involved in the many aspects of the brewing industry and just by doing it myself."*

ODELL BREWING COMPANY

"Make a difference and touch people"
Melanie Parks, Blooming Property Management

◆

BACKGROUND

Melanie Parks of Park City, Utah, established *Blooming Property Management* in 1978. Today she has over 50 employees primarily focused in the real estate and property management field. Prior to *Blooming Property Management*, she once owned a movie theater and a small landscaping company. Melanie still owns a working ranch, raising quarter horses, and it continues to be one of her greatest passions.

INTERVIEW

Q: What was your initial startup cost and source?

A: $0, we bootstrapped from the start by first offering landscaping and cleaning services.

Q: Did you use a business plan?

A: No.

Q: The vision of the company and the community you serve? Which came first, the problem or the idea/solution?

A: I started out gardening, landscaping, and cleaning for my clients. I started asking if I could do other things for them. A few of them asked if I could watch their home while they were away. My desire was to be able to give homeowners freedom to come own in Park City, go skiing and not have to worry about fixing their vacation home while they were away. I took the kind of care for their homes as is they were my own. Property managers didn't exist when I arrived in Park City, and the need for property management services for vacation homeowners was obvious to me. I wanted to create something as a nucleus business where we could offer 401Ks, insurance, all the stability and reasons why people

MELANIE PARKS

work for larger companies.

Q: Where do you see yourself and your company in 10 years?

A: I see Blooming Property Management being viewed as the model for other property management companies and to turn the business over to our employees, but still retain a percentage of the company.

Q: The genesis of the idea?

A: I found a need, filled that need, and my timing was perfect. I wanted to create year round jobs for myself and my employees, but didn't want to deal with the headaches of seasonal help, so I figured out a way to keep us employed year round by expanding my business.

Q: Biggest challenges? What do you know now that you wish you'd known sooner?

A: Handing over control, not doing all the work myself, and having other people do the work that needs to be done. Having people I could rely on to take care of our properties as well as I do. Creating a team where everyone is on the same page. I'm grateful that most of our employees have been with us for 15+ years. At one time, I did burn out and left my company in the hands of others who didn't have the same vision, the company started to go downhill fast. In focusing on the profit/loss balance sheets, I learned a valuable lesson that as a company grows, everything needs to be monitored more closely.

> *"In focusing on the profit/loss balance sheets, I learned a valuable lesson that as a company grows, everything needs to be monitored more closely."*

Q: What aspects of ownership are the most rewarding?

A: Realizing that I am making a difference for our clients, employees and myself. I really enjoy what I do. The money is an unexpected reward and was never the motivation. I appreciate the fact that I can enjoy my horse hobby which in itself is another business (albeit an expensive one) on the side.

Q: Are there one or two things you can attribute your success to? Luck, timing, someone who helped you?

A: Timing was definitely part of my success. I was inspired by a class I took to get off the ball and follow my dream. A real turning point in my life was that first skiing vacation in Park City, I knew this where I wanted to be, the people here really lit me up. I love beautiful homes and am a clean freak.

Q: How do you attract and retain the best employees? What is the most important attribute you look for?

A: I strongly support an employee ownership model. You don't need to have a college degree to work for me, and I prefer more natural people. I advance people for their hard work. If they fit well in our culture, there will always be a place they can move up to. I suggest starting at the bottom and working your way up. For other owners; promote from within your organization to people who have earned their stripes. An ability to work with others in a team is key.

Q: Can you recommend any training or resources such as books, classes, or websites? Do you recommend an MBA?

A: No on the MBA. Landmark Education helps people to discover who they really are. I recommend *Think and Grow Rich* by Napoleon Hill and *The Power of Now* by Eckhart Tolle. I'm a big believer in having a business/personal coach.

Q: Slogan to live by or what it might say on your tombstone?

A: "She made a difference and touched people." I believe that the most important thing is to have a strong spiritual belief; that there is a higher power you can rely on. Have faith that things are going to work out (they always do), just don't give up.

MELANIE PARKS

"The art of being wise is the art of knowing what to overlook."

- William James

"Life is short; we're not here for a long time,
we're here for a good time."
Bob Parsons of The Go Daddy Group, Inc.

◆

BACKGROUND

In 1997, Bob Parsons founded The Go Daddy Group, Inc., of which includes GoDaddy.com, the world's largest domain name registrar. As the sole developer and proprietor of the technology it uses, they proudly do not outsource or offshore any of their operations. Doing so has enabled Go Daddy to provide better support (24/7) and ensure the most advanced and competitively-priced products and services available today. The Go Daddy Group currently manages over 36 million domains. They offer a complete internet business product line, including comprehensive hosting solutions, web site creation tools, secure SSL certificates, personalized email with spam and anti-phishing filtering, e-commerce tools and more. Go Daddy has already received numerous awards and continues to be recognized for their achievements, to list them all would fill an entire chapter! To see the complete list, visit godaddy.com. The Go Daddy Group, Inc. is based in Scottsdale, Arizona and currently has over 2,170 employees.

INTERVIEW

Q: Prior entrepreneur experience?

A: In 1984, in my basement, I started Parsons Technology and we built software for small home businesses. I sold it in 1994 to Intuit for $64 million. I never had any other investors, and never borrowed any money.

Q: Initial startup cost of Go Daddy?

A: I started it from scratch and without a business plan, which is probably exactly the wrong thing to do, but my idea back then was born from the fact that I had a lot of money. I had all of this money from selling Parsons Technology and no idea. So the only thing I knew, back in '97, was that the Internet was really starting to gel and I wanted to be a part of it. I decided to hire a group of intelligent people, go getters, and try a bunch of things, discarding what didn't work and doing more of what did. What I didn't realize at the time was that it's a lot easier to find stuff that doesn't work than it is to find something that does. We tried all sorts of things.

We were an ISP, and learned you lose a lot of money doing that. We tried education, we built custom websites. None of it worked and I was the sole funding source. A term that was used back then, but you don't hear much anymore, was 'burn rate.' All internet companies were judged by their cash burn rate, ours was $300,000-$400,000 a month. Since I was writing the check for that burn rate, I was the one getting burned every month. That continued until October 2001 when the company finally turned the corner and became cash flow positive.

Before I moved out to Scottsdale to start the company, I got divorced, did the divide by two scenario, coming out with little more than $30 million after taxes. As the company was losing money, I mentally used to draw a line in the sand. I remember thinking 'I'm not going to get really worried about this business until I have only $25 million left. Then I'd get down to $25 million and I'd draw the line at $22 million and then $18 million and then $12, $10 and $8 million. What accelerated the drain? Like most people, I had a lot of money in the stock market, and when the dot bomb crash started happening, I got sucked right down the tubes with the market. At times, between what I lost in the business and what I lost

> *"Two other things that have helped me succeed are luck and perspective."*

in the stock market, was nearly two million dollars a month. All in all, I had lost somewhere between $15-$20 million.

There's an interesting story behind how we made the decision in 1999 to become a domain registrar, and that decision has made the company successful. We initially became a

THE GO DADDY GROUP INC.

registrar to simply sell our website software. When I was getting down to either make it or break it with the last of my funding, I had decided to get back to my roots, creating internet intellectual property in the form of website software where customers could build their own websites. I figured if we kept it cheap, under $30, we could sell thousands of them. We still have that product today, it's called Website Tonight and it's probably now in its 20th incarnation. We believed we could attract customers by being the lowest priced domain registrar, and offer the best service in the industry. At the time, our competitors customer service was horrible, and had rates upwards of $35-$70/year! We debuted our domain registration at $8.95 a year with an emphasis on superior customer service. It's still the mantra we live by today.

I was down to about $8 million in the bank and moving close to nothing. I made a decision in my mind to shut the company down while I had still had some money left.

I went to Hawaii to figure it all out. I never told anybody. I'm the type of guy who won't stick anybody no matter what, so I went there to figure out how to pay creditors, how to give employees severance and how to shut the business down gracefully. But while I was there, it just felt wrong to close the business down and the epiphany came when I went to get my car and there was a guy my age parking cars. I noticed he was really happy doing with what he was doing. And it hit me. I said to myself, if this business fails, the worst thing that can happen is I'll be parking cars, right? It was in that moment I decided that I was going to stick with the business no matter what.

> *"The trick is to accept the worst thing and start going at it one step at a time, one day at a time."*

business no matter what. I was broke before and happy as hell, I could be again, and I didn't need all that money to be happy. I figured if the company goes broke, I'll go broke with it. The following October (2001) the company turned the corner and was cash flow positive and has been ever since. I was that close. The Chinese have a saying and the saying is,

"The temptation to quit will be greatest just before you succeed."

Q: The passion that it fills for you personally?

A: Passion is paramount for me, and doing things my own way. I like to run an edgy company and I like to keep things fun. I like to reward my people very well. This past year (2008), other companies were telling their employees "we're having a bad year and cancelling our Christmas party because it's wrong for us to celebrate." Not us. We spent $1.75 million on our Christmas party! And you know what? For all the media criticizing me, I figure we received over $2 million worth of media value on the party alone. Here's what I told the media; I said "I could have taken that money and put it in my bank account and just told everyone; hey times are hard, we're not having a party this year." Well, last I heard recessions are caused by people not spending money, not by people throwing parties. We hired Joan Jett and the Black Hearts and .38 Special to perform. We gave away motorcycles, scooters, and half a million in cash. We rented Chase Field, where the Diamondbacks play and had a blast. While it certainly has been a good recruiting tool, it was more important to share our success with the employees who made it happen.

> *"... after you get your mind right with perspective the irrational fear goes away..."*

The Go Daddy Group Inc.

Q: Where do you see yourself & your company in 10 years?

A: I see ourselves standing along Google and Microsoft, at least that's my vision. We continue to grow. Our market share worldwide is now at 47%. In our industry we continue to be not only the largest company but the fastest growing. We own all the technology that we sell. We just opened a new facility in Amsterdam so we can better service Europe. I see us being one day, hopefully, the gatekeeper for the Internet.

Q: Looking back now, is there anything you wish you had done differently? What do you know now that you wish you'd known sooner?

A: Well, the only thing I would have done differently is I would have become a domain registrar sooner. I would have taken advantage of all the promotional things I found to work. For example, advertising on television, doing edgy commercials and reaching out in media other than the Internet to complement our efforts on the Internet. All those things that I've subsequently learned. Had I known them 10 years earlier, I'd be the king now.

Q: The genesis of the idea to become a domain registrar?

A: We started selling do-it-yourself website software, and every one needed a domain name in order to work so it would have an address for the website. We had to refer the customers to one of the few registrars back then such as Network Solutions, Registrar.com and others. Their prices were high and service horrific, add to that poor systems overall. So it was then that we said "hey, there's an opportunity here." We were warned at that time not to get into an industry already dominated by a couple of key companies. But we saw an opportunity to come in and have low prices and good service, that turned out to be as right as rain. That was the decision that made the company. But we never thought that we would make our niche being a domain registrar, but it certainly turned out that way.

Q: Was it hard to become a domain registrar?

A: First of all, to post all the bonds and stuff we needed and to develop the systems it was about a million bucks and took us about a year. It could have been done cheaper, but the reason it cost us that much is because we went in and did it the right way. But that's also one of the reasons why we were able to accelerate and grow the way we did, because we initially built a strong core infrastructure.

Q: Biggest rewards, what aspects of ownership have been the most rewarding?

A: The absolute biggest reward for me is to be able to do something right; to be able to do something right by our employees, to do something right by our community (we donate a

BOB PARSONS

lot of money into the community), to do something right by our customers, and have fun doing it. That is the absolute best reward. I absolutely love that and that's why to this day I'm still the only investor because I want to make sure that that continues.

Q: Are there one or two things you can attribute your success to, luck, and timing, someone who helped you?

A: After the dot com crash happened (in 2000), advertising became more affordable, and people who wouldn't even talk to us before were lining up at our door because we were one of the few companies paying our bills. But what really made the company was a decision we made years ago, and one we've continued to add to. To this day we're the only Internet company that I know of that operates like this and here it is, it's the secret to Go Daddy's success: People are at the core of everything we do. When it comes to transacting business, doing research, playing, communicating with others, shopping; people love to use the Internet. But when it comes to learning or solving problems people much prefer to deal with other people, right? So what we have done is made our primary goal to have service second to none. Call us anytime day or night and you'll get a really motivated individual. In our call centers, 40% of our staff have been with us for more than two years. And we pay them $18-20/hour vs. most other call centers that pay $8-10/hour.

Two other things that have helped me succeed are luck and perspective. Perspective to me is all about thinking the right way. I learned that when I was a combat marine in Vietnam. All the things that step through the rules, you know. For example, when I first got into Vietnam, I found out that I was a replacement for one of four guys that was killed a day or two earlier. The senior guy was only 19 and had been there for two and a half months. I thought for sure I was going to die and accepted that fact. I told myself the worst that can happen is I'm going to die, but until that happens I'm going to do my job as a Marine and my only goal was to live for mail call the next day.

THE GO DADDY GROUP INC.

I learned to do that back then and I did that with Parsons Technology. I did it in college and I've done it at Go Daddy. The trick is to accept the worst thing and start going at it one step at a time, one day at a time. If you keep doing that and hang in there, eventually luck is going to shine on you and make sure that when it does, you're smart enough to see it.

Q: So the right perspective and living in the moment has been vital to your success?

A: Yes. If you are constantly worried about what some guy is going to do to you or if something bad is going to happen to your business, then you spend all your energy trying to avoid those things. In doing so, you are never going to see the lucky break when it comes. So you've got to be in the moment as much as you can and that's where perspective comes into play.

Q: What about fear?

A: Everybody has a little fear, but what occurs is after you get your mind right with perspective the irrational fear goes away and you stay targeted on where you want to go, not dwelling on consequences or the worst thing that can happen. When you can quantify it and put it on a shelf, you can operate in the moment.

Q: How do you attract and retain the best and brightest employees? What is the most important attribute you look for?

A: Initially it took a whole lot of selling from our standpoint, and persuading employees of the opportunity here. But as time has gone by, since we're consistently voted one of the Best Places to Work here in Arizona and given our publicity, ad success, the edginess of the company, our parties, and all the other fringe benefits, our employees take care of the recruiting. Over 80% of our hires are referrals from current employees. But what do I personally look for? While the appropriate experience and education is important, the thing that I've always looked for and placed more emphasis on is somebody with a light in their eyes, you know? They want to make a difference, they're engaged, and when they get up, they want to come in and willing to do the work to make it

Bob Parsons

happen. That's the guy or gal I want to go to war with, and that's who I want to work with.

Q: So you want people who show up for more than a paycheck?
A: Exactly, people that want to make a difference.

Q: Your thoughts on the employee ownership model?
A: We have all kinds of rewards for our employees. From bonuses to fringe packages second to none. Our employees hold phantom options in the company when the company is realized, many of them will share in that success, and they understand that. Many know it's a reward and a thank you for going through hell with me, believing in the company, and sticking by me back when we had to all take pay cuts. There are others who have joined us subsequently who didn't go through that, yet have made a tremendous difference and are one of the reasons why we're as successful as we are. So I'm all for the employee ownership model.

Q: Do you recommend an MBA for an entrepreneur?
A: No I think it's a waste of time. I think the ability to write and express oneself in the written word is uncommon, and when it exists it's a beautiful thing. I don't boast about this too often, but the one thing I'll tell you; the best copywriter I know in this world is me.

Q: Do you suggest finding a good business coach? What about mentors?
A: No on the business coach, I believe you need to solve your own issues. I guess I have had a few mentors, people like Ulysses S. Grant, Sherman, Alexander the great. As you can see I'm a really military kind of guy. To a much lesser extent, however someone whom I have great respect for is

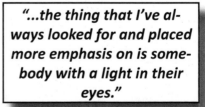

"...the thing that I've always looked for and placed more emphasis on is somebody with a light in their eyes."

Bill Gates. There are certain things he did that were really smart, for example, once you put a team on a product, it's never finished. You continue to push it and push it. That's

THE GO DADDY GROUP INC.

how back when he was at the helm, they got things like Excel and Word right eventually. We do that same thing here and it's a lesson well heeded. I also have tremendous respect for people like Oprah Winfrey, for all she's accomplished.

Q: Slogan to live by or what it might say on your tombstone?
A: Life is short brother, that's it. Life is short. My little brother says it best. He says, "We're not here for a long time. We're here for a good time."

Q: Is there anything else you want to share with an aspiring entrepreneur?
A: Start small, build a solid foundation and continue to improve it each and every day. Not long ago I was on the Donnie Deutsch Show with Susie Welch, Jack Welch's wife and this guy called in. He's working a day job and trying to do his business part-time. She told him that he should either quit his job and do it fulltime or quit the business, which is exactly the wrong thing to do. That's somebody that was telling it like it ain't, in my opinion, because this guy needs to get his business where he can continue to improve it until he finds the key on how to make it work. Once it starts working and he starts generating a profit then he should jump into it fulltime but you don't jump into something full-time, balls to the window when you don't have any resources or some backup. The year I quit my job and started working fulltime at Parsons Technology, I made $280,000. The next year I made $2.5 million and the next year I made $5 million. The idea to jump when this thing has no direction, makes no sense. It's like jumping in a pool with no water in it.

So my advice is always keep it covered, keep going, start it small, keep building it, get the foundation and find a way to make it work. And expect that to take 2-3 years as long as you keep at it. Eventually, if you have the right perspective in the company you will find a way to make it work if you love what you're doing. But staying covered may not be the easiest thing to do but that enables it all to happen. I was able to do that the first time with Parsons Technology because I had a real job. I didn't do what Susie Welch said, and quit. The

BOB PARSONS

second time I was able to do it because I had over $30 million in cash. I almost lost it all but I still had that as my bolster.

Authors note:
Be sure to check out Bob's 'Sixteen Rules'
in *Appendix F*.

"My biggest fear in life was to die doing work without meaning or impact. Don't waste your time in a vocation you don't enjoy. If you woke up and were told 'Today is the last day of your life', would you go to work? If the answer is no, then you're in the wrong job."
Jon Payne, Western Air Enterprises

◆

BACKGROUND

Jon Payne is co-owner of Western Air Enterprises (Western Air Flight Academy) located in Broomfield, Colorado. He has no prior experience in this field but was the former CIO of Wild Oats Markets in Boulder, Colorado.

INTERVIEW

Q: What was your initial startup cost and source of funding?
A: $250,000 in personal savings.

Q: How long until there was a positive cash flow?
A: It was an existing business that already had positive cash flow.

Q: Did you use a business plan?
A: Yes, in a sense, as I reviewed the last five years of tax returns of the business before becoming a partner in it. That said, I am not a big fan of large complex planning documents because they tend to paralyze you into inaction.

Q: What is the vision of the company and the community you serve?
A: To enable anyone who has a desire to fly the ability to do so, that's the flight instruction side. To give people the "freedom of flight" - to go anywhere they want without limits.

Q: What is the passion that it fills for you personally?

A: I did a "discovery" flight with another school six years ago. Today I'm a commercial pilot, flight instructor, aircraft owner and am running a flight school! I have always had a real passion for aviation and I love to share the experience of flight with others. The really amazing thing is that this doesn't feel like work to me, even on those so-called bad days.

Q: What was the genesis of the idea?

A: I have always been into aviation since I was a kid, I built and flew model airplanes, grew up near an airport, and my father and uncle were pilots. I remember dreaming of flying for the Air Force, but my eyesight ruled that out early, and I made up lots of excuses as to why the idea of flying at all wasn't realistic or practical. Instead, I fell into the path of doing what I felt was right to do to "earn a real living." As it turns out, I chose information technology as a vocation, I was successful at it, enjoyed the work and the challenges that went with it. In 2001, leveraging a decent severance package from Qwest, and with our kids off in college, I had the time and financial means to consider where my life was going next. When I took that ride in a Cessna 172 after 20 years away from general aviation, I was hooked from the time the engine started. I began attending the flight school and pursuing my pilot's license. A few years later, I bought my first plane.

> *"I have always had a real passion for aviation, and I love to share the experience of flight with others."*

Q: Where do you see yourself and your company in 10 years?

A: Here. I love what I do and would gladly do it seven days a week, but I don't have to. I just see the company being larger and me having the ability to fly more. I am only a few years from the typical retirement age, but have found what I want to do!

Q: What were your biggest challenges?

A: Fuel prices, cash flow and the weather because Colorado winters slow down business. Staff development is a biggie –

finding the people that can afford the job. Also, making the shift from a small company to a larger enterprise.

Q: What were the biggest rewards?

A: Being able to do what I truly love and make a decent living at it. Being in a plane is like "a desk with a view." I used to have a nice window view of the Boulder flatirons from my old desk. No contest; the view from the cockpit beats it hands down.

> *"Some of the smartest business people I know didn't attend college."*

Q: Are there one or two things you can attribute your success to?

A: Becoming a better listener, honesty, integrity, and fairness.

Q: What is the most important attribute you look for in an employee?

A: I look for a passion for flying and teaching and a willingness to continuously learn.

Q: Can you recommend any training or resources such as books, classes, or websites? Do you recommend an MBA?

A: *Free to Choose* by Milton Friedman and any book by Gary Hamel. I have an MBA and I think it doesn't hurt to have one since I am tapping into a bit of that knowledge now. However, some of the smartest business people I know didn't attend college. I discovered late in my career the power of networking, "life is not an individual sport".

Q: What is your slogan to live by or what it might say on your tombstone?

A: My biggest fear in life was to die doing work without meaning or impact. Don't waste your time in a vocation you don't enjoy. If you woke up and were told "Today is the last day of your life"' would you choose to work? If the answer is no, then you're in the wrong job.

JON PAYNE

"To know, is to know that you know nothing. That is the meaning of true knowledge."

- Confucius

*"Your attitude is the mind's paintbrush,
it can color any situation."*
Lynne Pittard, Visual Arts Network

◆

BACKGROUND

Lynne Pittard, of Lake Worth, Florida, launched Visual Arts Television Network via IPTV and Sky Angel Satellite system on Sept. 15, 2007. The broadcasting entertainment company began with five employees and is growing. The idea for the network happened over twenty years ago as she talked with other artists about the need for a network dedicated to the visual arts. Her interest in art began, at the age of thirty four, from an art show on PBS that offered oil painting instruction. She was inspired to learn to paint and within two years she had her own TV show teaching painting. For more than twenty-five years, Lynne has been living her dream and sharing her passion for painting by teaching others to paint. Her current goal is to bring entertaining visual arts programming to every generation through her TV network dedicated to the arts. She believes exposure and appreciation of the arts helps bring people back to the "real" world and will strengthen our culture and family units. She hosted and starred in over 130 of her own half hour television shows on PBS that were aired for over 20 years. She has written eight instructional books and has her art work licensed and published around the world.

INTERVIEW

Q: What was your initial startup cost and source?

A: The initial $250,000 was secured from my husband and my personal assets accumulated over 43 years together. We invested everything we could through mortgages, credit cards and cashing in our life insurance policies. Together this has been a walk of faith as we pursue our dream. Thirty friends and family invested $10,000 increments for a total of $500,000 and became equity holders of the startup network

LYNNE PITTARD

in a pre-launch private offering.

Q: How long until there is a positive cash flow?

A: Hopefully soon! Operating as a startup network since late 2007, the network has negotiated with major carriers , we expanded our management team and established dozens of needed affiliates and professionals for programming and operations. The release of additional company equity in a second offering to investors will enable us to secure up to $10 million to move forward. The operating capital is needed for staffing, securing a satellite provider to send our signal to major cable and satellite systems and expand the programming content. Within three years we project the revenues streams from carriers and sales of our commercial spots will provide the positive cash flow and offer a substantial ROI to our investors.

Q: Did you use a business plan?

A: Yes. From the first months of the company we retained a top legal firm to provide legal guidance. Their expertise and guidelines in creating a great business plan and offering memorandum provided the best foundation for the future and success of the network.

Q: Have you had to morph your original business plan to meet the demands of the market?

A: We've made adjustments since it was first written; taking input from others to help slant to the needs of the larger investors. We've made great progress so far with little funding and feel prepared to weather the challenges of the current economy crisis

Q: What was the genesis of the idea?

A: Twenty years ago at an arts industry trade show, I was speaking with other TV artists on the limited timeslots available to us on TV. We all expressed the need for a visual art network that could inspire creativity in others and entertain them. I want to create this specialty network that offers diverse art forms to all generations and to serve as an artist's advocate. The arts industry makes it hard for creative individuals to financially support themselves because there's very little focus on the financial side. My goal is to leverage our model to help artist own the rights to their own work and shows. I want to give the arts industry advertisers the ability to reach their target audience and endorse or sponsor an artist.

Q: What is the vision of the company and the community you serve?

A: To offer true visual arts content that networks like Bravo, A&E, and PBS have neglected in favor of performing arts. Advancements in technology in broadcasting have opened up new opportunity for niche players like us. There has never been a network focused solely on the visual arts. We believe our target market of advertisers is largely untapped: museums, galleries, schools, and travel opportunities for artists. The current option for advertisers to reach their market audience is only through very pricey art magazine ads.

Q: What is the passion that it fills for you personally?

A: To provide an outlet for artists to reach out to a worldwide audience, share their creativity, talents and their own passion for the visual arts.

Q: Where do you see yourself and your company in 10 years?

A: Within 10 years, my personal goal is to contribute my resources to work with a foundation that is focused on art therapy that helps Autistic and Alzheimer's patients be restored to productive lifestyles. I see the company as the leader in visual arts with wholesome family entertainment and inspiring programs. This is not at all where I imagined I would be at the age of 60,

> *"I know deep inside that this is my calling and purpose; it is my opportunity to contribute to society and leave a legacy that will continue to inspire..."*

but I know deep inside that this is my calling and purpose; it is my opportunity to contribute to society and leave a legacy that will continue to inspire creativity in others for generations to come. I plan to stay involved in the project and find

LYNNE PITTARD

the right investors and management team to ensure the network keeps it focus and vision. My biggest concern is the loss of the vision and mission in the future. A&E and Bravo were arts networks that sold for huge profits, the new owners and management abandoned the arts to pursue other programming.

Q: What were your biggest challenges? What do you know now that you wish you'd known sooner?

A: Biggest challenges were learning about all the new industries involved, the time needed to network and secure affiliates in all areas of growth and being very undercapitalized. I would have secured a CFO and a financial advisor sooner. Once

> *"Once I opened up and asked for help, things changed for the better."*

I opened up and asked for help, things changed for the better. Reaching out to qualified advisors and coaches allowed me to gain confidence as a new CEO. In the beginning, passion and enthusiasm kept me focused. As challenges and roadblocks evolved, I wish I had felt more self confident as a leader and realized that I was capable to take on the task ahead of me.

Q: What have been your biggest rewards? Any unexpected rewards?

A: The biggest reward is the support of friends and family who caught my vision, and took a financial risk to join in. Now I share my excitement with those I love as we grow the network. As founder, a big reward is having new affiliates believe in and support the network. They see what the network can be. I'm blessed to work with many creative individuals. The day we received a call from DreamWorks about airing their art movies in our prime time, I knew we had something special. Art is my passion and now I can share this love with others worldwide.

Q: Are there one or two things you can attribute your success to? Was it luck, timing, someone who helped you?

A: My faith, a desire to learn, a positive attitude and being de-

VISUAL ARTS NETWORK

termined were all keys to my success. My husband of forty-three years inspired me to emerge from a quiet and shy housewife to what I am today. I am so very grateful that he supported me and works with me in fulfilling my vision and chasing my dream.

Q: How do you attract and retain the best employees? What is the most important attribute you look for? What are your thoughts on the employee-ownership model?

A: To attract the best, we offer good benefits, allow for creative expression, and provide a positive atmosphere. I look for honesty and good work ethics. I look for creativity and passion, and I am an advocate of employee ownership.

Q: Any recommended training and resources? Books, classes, websites? Do you recommend an MBA?

A: No on the MBA as a requirement for success. Success can be based on your passion, desire to work and do your best. I had no formal training in the arts and became a national TV artist in a very short time and ran a successful art business for over 25 years. As the CEO of a TV network, I wish I had taken more computer classes and basic skills in running a business. On the job training is a challenging way to run a large company.

> *"My faith, a desire to learn, a positive attitude and being determined were all keys to my success."*

Q: Slogan to live by or what it might say on your tombstone?

A: "Commit to the Lord whatever you do and all your plans will succeed." - Prov. 16:3. "The task ahead of you is never as great as the power behind you." - Mathew 17:20.

Q: Anything else you want to add?

A: Until I discovered the arts at the age of thirty-four, I did not know my own identity. I never knew I had such a power within. I said a prayer that I wanted to make a difference in the world. That God would use me to touch people's lives in a special way, and show them the beauty in world. With-

LYNNE PITTARD

in a few weeks I saw my first oil painting show on TV that changed my life. I strive to make a difference in this world and leave a legacy to others. We all need a focus outside of ourselves and we can be greater than anything that can happen to us. With God all things are possible, and I know He is in control because of the miracles I have seen along my walk of faith.

41

*"Life's intensity of spirit rests on a pinpoint
and it hurts staying there."*

The Pond Guy

BACKGROUND

'The Pond Guy', who wishes to remain anonymous, started a pond landscaping company in 2006 and uses 2-3 contractors. He had no prior landscaping experience and had worked for a large multinational corporation for years prior. He spends his summers in Colorado and his winters in Mexico. He makes more than enough income in the summer to last him well through the winter where he spends most of his time sailing and hanging out with his boat cruising friends, living the kind of life you probably imagine when listening to a Jimmy Buffett song.

INTERVIEW

Q: What was your initial startup cost?
A: $3,000, personal savings.

Q: How long until you had reached a positive cash flow?
A: Two months.

Q: Did you use a business plan?
A: I didn't write a formal plan.

Q:What was the genesis of the idea?
A: I first built a pond for my wife, and then told the local pond supply company I wanted to build ponds for others. They referred more business to me than I could handle. I wanted a business that would allow me to live in Mexico in the winter and in Colorado in the summer. This business has allowed me to do that for the past 3 years.

Q: What came first, the problem or the solution?

A: It was a need that wasn't being met. I maintain, build, and fix all types of ponds. Many people have me take care of their ponds while they are on vacation.

Q: The passion that it fills for you personally?
A: Having an outlet of self-expression for my creativity. I enjoy my customers and the people I work with.

Q: Where do you see yourself and your company in 10 years?
A: Perhaps having one or two full time contractors, but keeping it small. I'd like to be doing something else. What that is, I don't know.

Q: Looking back now, is there anything you wish you had done differently?
A: I wish I would have started sooner and hired someone else to help me. Taking better care of myself physically would have been a good idea for this job.

Q: Biggest rewards?
A: The money is good, better than I expected. I have great personal relationships I've made through the business.

Q: How do you attract and retain the best employees? What is the most important attribute you look for?
A: The ideal candidate is knowledgeable, personable, and reliable. In our business those are extremely rare attributes you come across. The contractors I do use tend to work out better when I give them independence on the projects I hire them for.

> *"When I started to apply the teachings of the Tao, things really begin to fall into place."*

Q: Are there one or two things you can attribute your success to?
A: When I started to apply the teachings of the Tao, things really begin to fall into place. Some examples are; 'to let things be,' 'if you create it in your mind and concentrate on it, you'll eventually manifest it,' and 'if you think you can, you will.' Also, finding good partners that are reliable (something rare

in the landscaping business).

Q: Can you recommend any training or resources such as books, classes, or websites? Do you recommend an MBA?

A: Yes on the MBA, anything that helps you run your business better. Wayne Dyer and his interpretations of the teachings of the Tao. The book *Markings* by Dag Hammarskjold. Any sales courses that teach you how to be a good listener and improve your communication skills.

Q: Slogan to live by or what it might say on your tombstone?

A: "Life's intensity of spirit rests on a pinpoint and it hurts staying there," by Dag Hammarskjold.

Q: Anything else?

A: People have to stay focused on what it is they want and truly believe that they can get it. As soon as you say you can't do something, you eliminate the chances of it becoming true for you. Traveling around the world is really important to gain valuable new perspectives, and when I come back from Mexico, it takes me about a month to readjust to the faster tempo of the USA. Lastly, don't set your goals in stone; enjoy the journey and listen to the wisdom of the Tao.

> *"People have to stay focused on what it is they want and truly believe that they can get it."*

THE POND GUY

"We act as though comfort and luxury were the chief requirements of life, when all we need to make us happy is something to be enthusiastic about."

- Charles Kingsley

42

"If you don't know where you are going, it matters not the decisions you make along the way."
Gary Rogers, Real Estate Sales and Productivity Coach

◆

BACKGROUND

Gary Rogers has built a business, his first venture as an entrepreneur, by combining two of his favorite passions: real estate and coaching. Based in Fort Collins, Colorado, Gary began his journey into real estate in 1999. As a Certified Real Estate Sales Professional, Gary established himself as an agent who had mastered the art of productivity in both real estate and life. With that firm foundation in education, and a desire to teach others, he now coaches others to overcome their own limitations. He believes that your thoughts control your actions, and you control your thoughts. He attributes his success to questioning and persistence. He thinks the breakthroughs come from keeping the focus on the end goal, and not on the obstacles. The slogan he loves is, "Move the rock, and make progress on whatever you do." Gary's rewards come from seeing his coaching clients "get it" after they have struggled with something awhile, and as a real estate agent, actually helping people find not just a house, but a home; a place where memories are made and families are raised.

INTERVIEW

Q: What was your initial startup cost and source?
A: $5,000 which was used from personal savings.

Q: How long until there was a positive cash flow?
A: Nine months

Q: Did you use a business plan?
A: No, not initially.

Q: What was the genesis of the idea?

A: For real estate sales: to get away from being managed by people with little or no people skills. For productivity coaching: I loved training and coaching, and wanted to help others.

Q: What is the vision of the company and the community you serve? What came first, the problem or the solution?

A: The community I serve is professionals wanting to get better at real estate, and people needing help with buying or selling real estate. The opportunity to coach came about because I had a strong desire to teach and coach. I knew what I wanted to do; I just didn't know where, how, with whom, or what the job would look like. Eventually, I connected with a leading real estate firm, and was exploring other opportunities with them. Together, we discovered they had a need for someone to do what I dreamt of doing. Through the process of matching ideas with their team, I was able to create a position that fulfilled what I wanted, and filled a need they had. By knowing what I wanted, the opportunity eventually presented itself.

Q: What is the passion that it fills for you personally?

A: Helping other people.

Q: Where do you see yourself and your company in 10 years?

A: Maybe three employees/partners, and enough passive income, so that I don't have to work if I don't want to.

Q: What were your biggest challenges? What do you know now that you wish you'd known sooner?

A: The biggest challenge in real estate initially was the inconsistency of a paycheck. The biggest challenge in coaching is helping people break free of their self-limiting beliefs. I wish I had learned sooner to free myself of self-limiting beliefs. I wish I had learned earlier that our thoughts control our actions, and we control our thoughts.

> *"Move the rock, and make progress on whatever you do."*

Q: What were your biggest rewards? Were there any unexpected rewards?

A: On the coaching side of my business, the biggest rewards are seeing people "get it" after they have struggled with something awhile. In real estate, I used to think I was help-ing people buy a house, and later I realized it is more than that. I was helping people buy a home; a place where memories are made, and families are raised.

> *"I knew what I wanted to do; I just didn't know where, how, with whom, or what the job would look like."*

Q: Are there one or two things you can attribute your success to? Was it luck, timing, someone who helped you?

A: I attribute my success to questioning, and persistence. I ask a lot of questions, and I really like to get a sense of the "why" of things. By asking a lot of questions, I typically find that the real answer is different than I initially thought. And, a lot of times the better questions come later in the process, and are questions that I didn't even originally think of. I think it helps to not be attached to the end result. The breakthroughs come from keeping the focus on the end goal, and not on the obstacles.

Q: How do you attract and retain the best employees? What is the most important attribute you look for? What are your thoughts on the employee-ownership model?

A: I feel my former company had a great model: the employees are the owners. The ownership part of the model creates a level of accountability, and a sense of pride that exempli-fies a "we" and not a "we/they" mentality. It is critical to have a culture which empowers everyone to feel they are making an important contribution. To attract and retain the best employees: 1) Clearly define the position; hire based on skills and abilities. 2) Regularly train, and regularly challenge. 3) Provide feedback, and get feedback.

Q: Any recommended training and resources? Books, classes, websites? Do you recommend an MBA?

A: *The Psychology of Achievement* by Brian Tracy is a fantastic resource. I do recommend an MBA because I think education

GARY ROGERS

is one of the few things that can't be taken from you. I don't believe that a degree necessarily means you are qualified to do anything. I highly recommend classes or books related to goal setting and achieving, and dealing with difficult people. I am a big believer in personality profiling to help understand how people might see us, and how we might better interact with those personalities that are different than our own.

> *"The breakthroughs come from keeping the focus on the end goal, and not on the obstacles."*

Q: Slogan to live by or what it might say on your tombstone?

A: The slogan I love: "Move the rock, and make progress on whatever you do." The slogan that guides me: "If you don't know where you are going, it matters not the decisions you make along the way." What I hope it says on my tombstone: "He made a difference."

Q: Is there anything else?

A: If you pursue something with enough passion, you will find fulfillment and success. Fulfillment is a choice. Be doggedly persistent in your pursuits.

43

*"He believed in himself,
his abilities and his dreams."*
Chris Roth, JobSite Tools, Inc.

◆

BACKGROUND
Chris Roth had a lawn mowing business when he was a young man. He worked his way through college by working in the oilfield, roofing, painting, and basement remodeling and finishing work. He also got involved in some multi-level marketing programs. He worked in the Telecomm industry and ended work there as a Regional Sales Manager, covering 14 states and four Canadian Provinces. Chris is the founder of JobSite Tools, Inc., a company that bought out JobData, Inc.

INTERVIEW
Q: What was your initial startup cost and source of funding?
A: With all investments, it was close to $750,000. All funds have come from JobData, Inc.'s investors, friends, family and my retirement plans.

Q: How long until there was a positive cash flow?
A: I am hoping that I will be bringing in positive cash flow by the end of the second quarter of 2009.

Q: Did you use a business plan?
A: Yes.

Q: Have you had to morph your original business plan to meet the demands of the market?
A: I wrote up a business plan before I took over JobData, Inc. This was my first direction on where I wanted to take the company and how I planned on getting there. The morphing of the business plan is based on two things, (1) learning what investor's need to see to make an educated decision on investing in the company; and (2) how our company will

CHRIS ROTH

205

use this business plan to lay out the strategic path we plan to follow. There will always be changes to the business plan as the market demands and needs change. For example, the market is now demanding that Project Managers/Foremen can track accidents by job. This change was made to the plan and will be released in the next version of the product.

Q: What was the genesis of the idea?

A: My former partner, Tim Cuneo, actually came up with the original idea. This came from his work with contractors and wanting to help them control their businesses, thus helping him with his. When he showed me what he was thinking about, I was hooked. With his experience on the distributor side of business and mine in working in different construction industries and with different contractors, the idea has just kept growing to what it is now.

Q: What is the vision of the company and the community you serve? What came first, the problem or the solution?

A: The problem came first. I have worked with many types of construction companies and in many industries. Tim had extensive experience working more in the distribution of products used in the construction industry. He saw how unorganized many contractors are regarding materials management and project management. The main vision of the company is to bring technology to an industry that still does most of its work on the yellow note pad.

Q: What is the passion that it fills for you personally?

A: The ability to work for myself. I know how hard I work and what I can do for a company, so why not do it for my own company. The main passion is to help a huge industry control costs and gain control of projects and to show them how to increase productivity while reducing time and controlling costs. This company has given me ideas and ways in which I can help other industries.

Q: Where do you see yourself and your company in 10 years?

A: I feel that I will be able to develop this product and a few additional complimentary products to meet the needs of the small one-man contractor and do-it-yourself people to the largest contractors. I see my potential customers as anyone with a construction budget whether they are contractors, institutions such as universities that want to control their costs or the do-it-yourself people. My goal is to get these products ready and to market in the next year. I see gaining market share quickly and then have a large software company buying out JobSite Tools. There are many companies which these products do match-up with their own core business. This will either be someone like a Microsoft, a project management software company or an accounting software company. I see myself continually trying to find or invent products that will help others be better at what they do. I have many ideas now and I am sure that in ten years I will be doing the same type of things. In 10 years I expect to be financially stable and to be able to spend as much time with my family as I want. This is my main goal and what I work for, my family!

Q: What were your biggest challenges? Looking back now, is there anything you wish you had done differently?

A: I wish that I would not have tried to do everything by myself and/or with one part-time developer. I know that if I had to do it over again I would get enough investment that would sustain a team of developers and me for one full year. My lack of knowledge in software development has been a very big challenge. With a product like this, that I feel can change an industry; it is hard to trust people you don't know. The developer I have been working with is a

> *"I wish that I would not have tried to do everything by myself and/or with one part-time developer."*

fantastic man and one I do trust. He has another job, so he has not been able to help as much as I need him. If starting over, I would have enough money to hire him full-time. This could have helped bring the product to the industry at least one year earlier. I now know from experience that software development takes a lot of time, money and patience.

Q: What are your biggest rewards?

A: The first reward is spending time with my family. Family is what life is all about and being able to spend so much time with them has been incredibly rewarding in itself. Another large reward is the self-realization that anyone can do about anything. Hard work and determination really do go a long way and this is what I want to set as an example for my two boys.

Q: What aspects of ownership are the most rewarding?

A: Probably the most rewarding thing is that I am now able to spend time with my family. My previous sales jobs kept me away from them an absurd amount of time. Being able to have a vision and make it happen is also extremely rewarding.

Q: Any unexpected rewards?

A: The surprise that I am able to do a lot more than I ever thought I could. I have always had very high expectations of myself. From my father's teachings and leading by example, I have always known that hard work and determination can take you far. I have thrown myself into an industry (software) that I knew nothing about, and I am learning all the time. I know that I will succeed in this industry, also.

Q: Are there one or two things you can attribute your success to? Was it luck, timing, someone who helped you, etc?

A: Probably the biggest thing I can attribute to my success is my father. He had an incredible work ethic and was the most solid man I have seen in the business world. I remember growing up and always wanting to be like him and to earn the respect from others that he had earned. I feel lucky that I was able to work with Tim Cuneo and to eventually be given the opportunity to take over the idea and build this company. Endurance and the ability to keep a very positive attitude through all the ups and downs of the software development process. It is not always easy when everything takes so much longer then I expect it to.

Q: Can you recommend any training or resources such as books, classes, or websites?

A: Depending on the industry you are in, you will always be able to find books that will help you. For the business world I would recommend *The Art of War* by Sun Tzu; *In Search of Excellence* by Thomas J. Peters and Robert H. Waterman; and *How to Become a Rainmaker* by Jeffrey J. Fox. I like motivational books and books about how others have succeeded in their line of work, whether it is in business, sports or life.

Q: Do you recommend an MBA?

A: I feel any and all education is good and will definitely help. But there is nothing like real-life experiences – successes and failures to teach and guide you. I know it has become a bit of a cliché, but if you don't have any failures, you are not trying hard enough.

Q: What is your slogan to live by or what it might say on your tombstone?

A: Believe in yourself!!! Something that might be appropriate on my tombstone would be, "He believed in himself, his abilities and his dreams."

Q: Anything else you would like to add?

A: I would say that failure is always in your mind. No one wants to fail. This goes from the little leaguer that wants to catch a ball or make the game-winning hit, to the businessman, especially one that gets investment from family and friends. You cannot let this fear scare you away from making things happen. You have to use it as adrenaline to keep you going and working harder towards your goals. I have

> *"We live in the greatest country in the world and this is the best time in the history of the world for entrepreneurs to be successful."*

invested almost my entire savings on this venture. I am not as worried about my own money because I know I can make more money in the future. I want to make sure that I come through for all the investors. We live in the greatest country in the world and this is the best time in the history of the world for entrepreneurs to be successful.

CHRIS ROTH

"The law of work does seem utterly unfair - but there it is, and nothing can change it; the higher the pay in enjoyment the worker gets out of it, the higher shall be his pay in money also."

- Mark Twain

"Luck and Timing are Everything"
David Samuels, Esposito's Finest Quality Sausage Products

◆

BACKGROUND

David Samuels spent 14 years as a management consultant for several companies, including stints with Ernst and Young and Sapient, before being bitten by the entrepreneurial bug. In 2002, he bought Esposito Sausage, a gourmet Italian sausage manufacturing and distribution company based in Hell's Kitchen, New York City. Esposito's gourmet sausage is proudly served in many of the upscale establishments in New York City, including The Four Seasons, but they also ship all across the United States – even as far as Alaska. By Samuels' estimate, the value of the company has doubled since he took the reins seven years ago.

INTERVIEW

Q: What was the initial start up cost and source?

A: I had to pay quite a bit of money to buy the company from the heirs of the family. Some of that was for a lease and some of it was for the regular startup costs. If I had to estimate, I would say the cost was a couple million. The source was primarily the Small Business Administration. I used the small business loans available to us and the heirs of the family were required by the SBA to take a much, much smaller note. I borrowed in a structure similar to bridge loans from friends and family because my savings alone weren't enough to make up the difference, I created a plan to pay those loans off within 3 years. I just made my final payment on a seven year SBA loan and finally being debt free is a wonderful feeling.

Q: Did you use a business plan?

A: Yes. In order to get the loans, I needed to show how I was going to make the business profitable. I made some of the most complex spreadsheets I've ever made and I was able to talk through the spreadsheets perfectly. I look back at some of them now and I can't even figure out why I did certain calculations that I did, but they were right at the time. Beyond that, it was a very rudimentary plan, just showing how to manage the business and identifying how I could make sure cash flow was not only maintained, but growing to ensure that I could meet the loan payments every month. Once I was accomplishing that, I looked into growth in different areas that I couldn't have imagined before.

Q: What was the genesis of the idea?

A: I was doing my consulting gig, as I had been forever. Then, unfortunately, the tragedy of September 11th occurred. Along with that, one of my clients stopped all consulting projects. So for the first time ever, I had no job and no income – and to make matters worse, I was newly married with a baby on the way. I figured that the best way to ensure my job security was to run my own company and be my own boss.

Q: What is the vision of the company & the community you serve?

A: It's an old world type company with real Italian roots and we really try to maintain that old world flavor. We still do a many things by hand that most of the large companies around the country automate. We get a better product by doing it by hand. We couple that old world style with new age needs. We have a line of sausages that are all natural and antibiotic free. We strive to maintain the gourmet approach in our marketing.

> *"I figured that the best way to ensure my job security was to run my own company and be my own boss."*

Q: What is the passion that it satisfies for you personally?

A: To control my own destiny. To be living or dying – hopefully not literally dying – based on my good or bad decisions. And it feels really good to know that you can do that. We all think we can do anything, or at least have believed that, and it's good to know sometimes you can.

Esposito's Finest Quality Sausage Products

Q: Where do you see yourself & your company in 10 years?

A: Hopefully, far apart from each other. And by that, I mean that I hope to have put enough of a management structure in place where it can be running for me and providing an income for me so that I can move on to my next adventure.

Q: What were your biggest challenges? Looking back now, is there anything you wish you had done differently?

A: You don't really realize the challenge of finding good employees, retaining good employees, and handling employee problems until every one of them is 100% your problem. If someone gets injured on the job somebody else can handle it, but the bottom line is that when it's your company, it all comes down to you.

> *"...luck and timing are everything."*

Q: What were your biggest rewards? What aspects have been most rewarding and have there been any unexpected rewards?

A: I'm much more hands-on mechanically than I ever expected, but I enjoy that. I was pretty good at business when I started. Now I'm good at business and I'm good in the meat industry. But I think that the other unexpected reward is the great response from customers. People will write us hand-written letters, saying, "Thank God we found good Italian sausage – we can't get any here in..." North Carolina, or Texas, or wherever.

Q: Are there one or two things you can attribute your success to? Was it luck, timing, someone who helped you?

A: I think if I were to pick two things, I would probably pick education and work experience. Of course, luck and timing are everything, and I had a little bit of each coming in. The luck was that I knew someone who knew someone that knew this business was up for change of ownership. And the timing was that when the person who was managing the business for the heirs found out that she wasn't going to be able to buy the company, she quit on them. I had about two months of helping the heirs figure out how to run their accounting

DAVID SAMUELS

system. They were paying me a little stipend to do that because they knew about meat, but not about business. On their dime, I got a full education of their business. On day one of my ownership I had already been there two months and I really felt confident that this was the right decision and everything was going to work out great.

Q: How do you attract and retain the best employees and what is the most important attribute you look for?

A: That's been one of our biggest challenges. We're not hiring for a high skilled profession; we need people to cut the meat and stuff it into sausages. When we find someone that we feel really wants to grow with the company, then we'll either give bonuses or tell them to take their spouse or family out for a dinner on us. On top of that, for the office people, sales people and the managers, we offer education, 401(k) and health benefits.

Q: Any recommended training and resources? Books, classes, websites, etc..? Do you recommend an MBA?

A: I always recommend reading books. Your book, 50 Interviews, is very insightful. It's amazing what you can learn from the stories of others. Another book I love is *Built to Last: Successful Habits of Visionary Companies* by James C. Collins and Jerry I. Porras. It is very insightful and really helps you see what can make one company edge out another one and stay around after the other one fails. I have taken so many classes varying from real business modeling to the business approach of making a business plan, from accounting to flower design. I've literally gone to a floral design course just because if you go to different courses, you meet different people. You see how different ideas are formulated, different problems are solved and you never know when that knowledge will be helpful in your future life. As far as getting an MBA goes, I think it's all about timing. If you know you want to be an entrepreneur but you haven't found your passion yet, an

> *"To run a company successfully, you need to look at it in as complex a manner as possible."*

MBA might help you do that. But I don't think it's a necessity.

Q: What would it say on your tombstone?

A: That's a hard one. I once read that, "If you want to truly live you have to first attend your own funeral." Once you understand that it will all end, then you can be free of that and you can just look forward to the next day. But at other times I might tell you that it's easier to ask for forgiveness than to ask for permission. And in business especially, you may have to do something that could rub someone the wrong way in order to make sure that your product gets noticed. Apologize later, but do it first – because if you ask them for permission you might end up losing your opportunity.

Q: Anything else?

A: There's no such thing as a really simple business to run. There's always going to be a problem. And I think to run a company successfully, you need to look at it in as complex a manner as possible. When we formulate new products we don't only go on flavor profile. Flavor is obviously number one, but if it's not going to be profitable as a product or it has a bad shelf life, then we won't go forward with that idea. So you have to really look at these things in a complex manner even though, in the end, this business is pretty simple: grind meat, spice it up, stuff it into casing and you're done.

David Samuels

"You gain strength, courage and confidence by every experience in which you really stop to look fear in the face. You must do the thing you think you cannot do."

- Eleanor Roosevelt

"Be an active aggressive seeker of information"
Ben Sawyer, OOKKII

◆

BACKGROUND

Ben Sawyer, along with Chris Ho, is a founder of OOKKII. This is Ben's fourth business, but he considers OOKKII his first true startup. His first business was at the age of 15 when he posted bills (posters) on a college campus, and then he started a computer consulting company while in high school. Later he sold it and traveled the world. He spent two years in Taiwan and now is in college at Colorado State University. To pay the bills while he is in school, he started his third business, Tech Takeout.

INTERVIEW

Q: What was your initial startup cost and source of funding?

A: None, but I consider my investment in time, human capital, as my startup cost.

Q: How long until there was a positive cash flow?

A: No positive cash flow yet but getting very close.

Q: Did you use a business plan?

A: Yes.

Q: Have you had to morph your original business plan to meet the demands of the market?

A: We are on the third iteration of our business plan. When we won the Web 2.0 award in Taiwan from Institute for Information Industry, we didn't have a formal plan. We knew a business plan was a core requirement of the upcoming 'demo. com' event the company was attending, so we put one together.

Q: What was the genesis of the idea? What came first, the problem or the solution?

A: The problem was that personal finance is not fun and most people don't want to do it (this is a universal problem). None of the solutions out there found a way to make managing your finances fun, and they certainly didn't appeal to a younger audience. The real benefit OOKKII brings to society is finding a way to get young kids engaged in personal finance.

Q: What is the vision of the company and the community you serve?

A: OOKKII is one idea around a larger vision I am truly passionate about. That vision is to help people better manage their lives by giving them new points of feedback. In the case of OOKKII, it is feedback about their spending and saving habits. This "financial feedback" empowers them to make better decisions about how they spend their money. It's a community-driven resource that gets more valuable the larger it grows. My little brother needed a way to better manage his finances and make personal finance fun. OOKKII is putting better financial management in the hands of young people and making it fun!

Q: Where do you see yourself and your company in 10 years?

A: As the community grows, I see it expanding into a much larger model, a social web that others are using to build sites that provide new forms of feedback in all aspects of life. Also, we want to link local merchants with local buyers – based on a community feedback and connecting with others who share your same interests to see where they shop (and what they pay for the same things you want). I would love to see lots of little OOKKIIs and look forward to the innovation that follows.

Q: What is the passion that it fills for you personally?

A: I have always been fascinated by people and psychology. OOKKII fills this passion by giving me a way to explore the psychology of an entire community.

Q: What was your biggest challenge? Looking back now, is there

OOKKII

anything you wish you had done differently?

A: Taking those first steps – to stop talking about the idea, to stop planning and customizing and perfecting it before you take action. "Stop building it, and start running it!" Also, don't wait. Someone else will have the same idea and you will kick yourself for not going after it. I've learned that ideas have a limited shelf life, so you've got to act before they spoil.

> *"I've learned that ideas have a limited shelf life, so you've got to act before they spoil."*

Q: What is your biggest reward?

A: The personal fulfillment of building something from nothing. To have people interacting with something I am creating. I'd also love to make a difference and change the world.

Q: Are there one or two things you can attribute your success to? Was it luck, timing, someone who helped you, etc?

A: My dad was my role model as he too was an entrepreneur. I attribute my "global view" to the time I spent helping him be successful. Read, read, and read – I spend a lot of time on websites like *Hacker News*. I suggest you seek out communities on the internet because they are full of a lot of bright people. A Google search is only a starting point – you have to be aggressively curious and don't believe the first thing you read or the popular opinion.

Q: How do you attract and retain the best employees? What is the most important attribute you look for? Do you have any thoughts on the employee-ownership model?

A: The best way to attract talent is to have a high quality idea. Good people will be drawn to you and your idea. I try to grab people with a whiz bang idea and then letting them see for themselves the true value and purpose behind the idea. I've learned through this startup that you've got to be really good at tailoring your idea to your audience – finding a way to light a spark in the listener. In fact, I feel the best test for a good idea is that it can be slanted many different ways and appeal to many different groups.

BEN SAWYER

Q: Can you recommend any training or resources such as books, classes, or websites? Do you recommend an MBA?

A: No on the MBA, as it is just one asset. When choosing between college and starting a business, I highly recommend the latter so you can get some failures behind you. In doing so, you'll come to college with a much greater appreciation for the context of what you're learning. A book I go back to occasionally is *How to Win Friends & Influence People* by Dale Carnegie.

> *"I suggest you seek out communities on the internet because they are full of a lot of bright people."*

Q: What is your slogan to live by or what it might say on your tombstone?

A: "Be an active aggressive seeker of information." This quote is actually on my dad's tombstone.

OOKKII

"The more you share, the more powerful you become."

David Schwaab, Rebit Inc.

◆

BACKGROUND

In the late 70's, David Schwaab crashed a Hewlett-Packard (HP) users group. His boldness caught the eye of an individual who recruited him to work at a small software startup. He was employee number nine, and in choosing work over school, he helped grow the company to over 70 employees before it was acquired by HP in 1981. At HP, David spent the next two to four years enjoying life as an 'intrapreneur'. Wikipedia defines an intrapreneur as an employee "who focuses on innovation and creativity and who transforms a dream or an idea into a profitable venture, by operating within the organizational environment." In 1985, while still with HP, David cofounded an office product company which grew to become the second largest in Denver. Eventually purchased by BT Office Products in 1990, he then started a board game business, Ways with Words, with two friends. He helped write the business plan and get the product off the ground. In 1999, David then funded and assisted his brother-in-law to start an all-natural taffy shop in Old Town Sacramento, California. In 2005, David took an early retirement from HP and started Rebit in his basement with a couple of colleagues. Rebit offers external PC backup solutions.

INTERVIEW

Q: I understand that Rebit is still in the research and development stage and not yet making a profit. How long do you anticipate until you can reach a positive cash flow?

A: We are projecting a profit for 2009.

Q: Did you use a business plan?

A: Yes.

Q: Have you had to morph your original business plan to meet the demands of the market?

A: Yes, in a major sense. We've changed how we are taking the solution to the market.

Q: What was the genesis of the idea?

A: Software to do simple and automated backups didn't exist. We saw it as a major gap in the market, and something we felt could be done much better than was currently being done. The innovation was that we saw backup as a background application. It simply runs in the background and the user doesn't need to worry about it.

> *"Success came from focusing on my strengths and knowing my weaknesses, and partnering with those who are strong where I was weak."*

Q: What is the vision of the company, and the community you serve? What came first, the problem or the solution?

A: Rebit targets the need of a simple back-up solution for non-technical users. The problem came first. It was a lack of easy to use backup software for the typical home user.

Q: Where do you see yourself and your company in 10 years?

A: Most likely, I will be running another company in another industry.

Q: What is the passion that being an entrepreneur fills for you personally?

A: To meet the unmet needs of the market and make money doing it, and to have fun along the way! And, as was done for me, to set an example for others that it can certainly be done.

Q: What were your biggest and most unexpected rewards?

A: I truly enjoy the community I now work in, it's filled with people I admire. Rebit has grown far beyond the vision of the original founders. Benefiting from simple kindness of complete strangers, I attribute much of Rebit's success to the support of the Colorado technology community who have

ReBIT

embraced Rebit and the opportunity to unselfishly help it grow and even become part of it.

Q: What were your biggest challenges? What do you know now that you wish you had known sooner?

A: I try not to ever regret anything as they become great learning experiences, but for your readers I can outline three big key areas to think about:

1. Form as a Corporation from the beginning because it was time consuming to do it after we had formed as an LLC. We wanted to begin offering company shares to new employees.

2. Consider bringing more development resources on board sooner. We tried to make it with the resources we had and I believe it stalled our company for a year.

3. I learned that by bringing in someone else to run the company, and allowing them to bring along their own staff, we significantly increased our speed to the market and it helped us secure additional funding.

Q: Are there one or two things you can attribute your success to? Luck, timing, someone who helped you?

A: Success came from focusing on my strengths and knowing my weaknesses, and partnering with those who are strong where I was weak. Put yourself out there no matter what. My first break in life came when I 'crashed' an HP users group, and in doing so, was a standout that got noticed by someone in power who was impressed by my boldness. I credit much of Rebit's success to Bill Beierwaltes, of Colorado vNet, and his support in the beginning. Bill gave us our first office space when we outgrew my basement. Bill has believed in our idea from the beginning and in doing so has given us credibility in the community.

DAVID SCHWAAB

Q: What are your strongest core beliefs?

A: Be open to other people, to new ideas and new ways of doing things. Be open to yourself and be optimistic. All businesses are a game played by the same rules. I've run successful ventures in a wide variety of different industries. Along the way I've learned the common elements that make any business successful.

> *"Expect the best results from yourself and others, and do whatever it takes."*

Q: Your thoughts on the employee-ownership model?

A: I'm a firm believer in the shared ownership model. It is how you get the best talent and get everyone accountable for the cumulative success of the team, or company.

Q: Do you recommend an MBA?

A: I believe in hiring MBAs, as they make great employees. As far as an entrepreneur having an MBA, you have to ask yourself why you think it would be necessary. There's no magic answer out there – you just need to do whatever it takes and empower others because you can't do it all by yourself. If you always expect the best from others and from yourself, that's what you'll get.

Q: Slogan to live by or what it might say on your tombstone?

A: What drives me is knowing I am making a positive difference in the world. Expect the best results from yourself and others, and do whatever it takes. On my tombstone I'd like it to say, "Be a good person," and "The more you share, the more powerful you become."

ReBIT

47

"Stick with it!"
Henry Schwartz, Trade Alert

◆

BACKGROUND

Henry Schwartz founded Trade Alert, a financial services firm in New York City in 2005. Henry currently has four employees. An entrepreneur from a young age, he delivered newspapers and sold candy, chewing tobacco and fireworks from his junior high school locker. Henry also had a business printing T-shirts while attending college. Trade Alert uses proprietary software to process high-speed market data and notify subscribers of market activity relevant to their business in real-time. Their tools are used by top Wall Street firms to supplement in-house systems and fill a significant need for a growing number of sales and trading professionals involved in electronic markets. Henry has traded on several US and European exchanges and led trading and development teams at The Hull Group, Salomon Brothers, Bear Stearns and Banc of America Securities. He and his partner William Sterling bring 30 years experience in derivatives trading and technology from exchange floors and small proprietary operations to the largest derivative desks on Wall Street. Together they bring unique insight into the challenges and demands presented by today's automated and fragmented markets, key to the innovative and efficient tools Trade Alert provides.

INTERVIEW

Q: What was your initial startup cost and source of funding?
A: Savings of $150K.

Q: How long until there was a positive cash flow?
A: One year.

Q: Did you use a business plan?
A: Yes, but I morphed it a little bit. It was good to have the plan to get started although it was a lot of work.

Q: What is the vision of the company and the community you serve? What came first, the problem or the solution?

A: The problem exists. We provide information tools to the stock market professionals who are facing an increasingly electronic and fragmented securities market. While we are currently focused on options and stock trading, we know our tool could work for futures, currencies, and energy. Our tool brings real-time data processing to the individual investor in a cost effective manner.

Q: What is the passion that it fills for you personally?

A: Addressing a challenging need with a very smart approach. I like being involved in markets and providing powerful tools for others to utilize in trading.

Q: What was the genesis of the idea?

A: The "idea" was the outgrowth of an existing idea that was never fully realized on a smaller scale, but made sense when serving hundreds of clients.

Q: Where do you see yourself and your company in 10 years?

A: Not here. Hopefully Trade Alert will be sold off and I'll be doing something else.

Q: What is your biggest challenge? Looking back now, is there anything you wish you had done differently?

A: Not only prioritizing which ideas to pursue, but tactically selecting which strategies and activities would lead to the highest returns. It's extremely important to select the best things to work on that move the idea forward. With so many things to do on your mind, the challenge is focusing on one idea and starting it off well before moving onto the next idea. It has to be the best thing for you to work on at the moment. At the previous companies where I worked, I learned how not to hire people. I suggest hiring people smarter than you. The cash flow at Trade Alert hasn't been much of a problem due to my initial up-

> *"It's extremely important to select the best things to work on that move the idea forward."*

front investment. While liberating, being held fully responsible for my own actions, can be challenging at times.

Q: What is your biggest reward? What aspects of ownership are the most rewarding? Were there any unexpected rewards? Any regrets?

A: Not needing to answer to any other investors. I don't have to please anyone but myself. An unexpected reward has been the direct appreciation I get from our clients. Having control has been a big reward. Being able to do what you want without it being solely about the money; the money will come eventu-

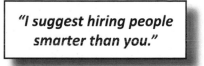

"I suggest hiring people smarter than you."

ally, but it is not the focus of everything I work on at Trade Alert. When I worked for other companies, it was always about money all the time. Having the freedom to make my own choices and pursue whatever I want is a big reward. One of my regrets would be that I should have started my business ten years ago, but it never seemed like it was the right time to leave my job. I realize now I could have created the circumstances to make this happen sooner.

Q: Are there one or two things you can attribute your success to? Was it luck, timing, someone who helped you, etc.?

A: I hooked up with a key software developer. By having a solid team on board with the basics of the idea, the team was able to understand where the company was starting and could see the incremental progress as it slowly evolved. I was committed to progress and strived to make Trade Alert as good as I knew it could be. Being able to determine the market need for your idea and then adapt your idea as necessary. I picked a market I knew very well after 15 years. I knew the market I was going into better than anyone. I think you are at a big disadvantage when you go into a market you know nothing about.

Q: How do you attract and retain the best employees? What is the most important attribute you look for?

A: I always look for the smartest people I can find as well as

HENRY SCHWARTZ

people I want to work with. I look for others who are passionate for the idea and understand how our clients are using our solution to help them do their job better. Empowering employees allows them to get better at their jobs.

Q: What training and resources would you recommend? Do you recommend an MBA?

A: Although I do have an MBA, I wouldn't recommend it. An MBA should not be pursued until you have clarified your vision as far as what you want to do. I was fortunate that my employer paid for it. I'm a believer in spending time with peers in similar situations. Having someone to talk to about

> *"I'm a believer in spending time with peers in similar situations."*

what you are going through has helped tremendously. This idea extends to having advisors to help you. My friend Dave, a very successful entrepreneur, was in a young entrepreneur's network which worked very well for him. It's helpful to seek access to people you can consult with. They'll help you develop new ideas and introduce you to others who will become important to your success. The quality of your network will, in a large part, determine your success. For example, use only trusted recommendations and find a good accountant.

TRADE ALERT

Q: What is your slogan to live by or what might it say on your tombstone?

A: "Stick with it," whether running marathons or in business, success is inevitable if you stick it out. I've learned it's the only way to get there. There are no short cuts.

"When in doubt, go higher."
Greg Shields, Concentrated Technology

◆

BACKGROUND

Greg Shields, is an independent author, instructor, and an IT consultant based in Denver, Colorado, and a cofounder of Concentrated Technology. With nearly 15 years of experience in information technology, Greg has developed extensive experience in systems administration, engineering, and architecture specializing in Microsoft systems management, remote application, and virtualization technologies. Greg is a Contributing Editor for TechNet Magazine and is the author of five books, including *Windows Server 2008: What's New/What's Changed*. Greg is also a highly sought-after instructor and speaker, speaking regularly at conferences like TechMentor Events, and producing computer-based training curriculum for CBT Nuggets. Greg is a recipient of Microsoft's "Most Valuable Professional" award with a specialization in Windows Terminal Services.

GREG SHIELDS

INTERVIEW

Q: How long did it take you to earn enough income to pursue your passion full-time?

A: It took me about three years. I stayed at my former job until I had built up enough work to chase this full-time.

Q: Did you use a business plan?

A: No.

Q: How did you get your start? What do you feel was the tipping point when you felt confident enough to take the risk and go out on your own?

A: From the age of 15, I was heavily involved in Kiwanis. I was in a high power position in the world-wide college version of Kiwanis. Throughout high school and college, Kiwanis gave me my first opportunities to speak, lead, write, and teach.

"A salary provides no incentive to excel."

Ever since then, I have always wanted to pursue writing and speaking full-time, but something was holding me back from making the jump full-time. But after attending several conferences, I realized I could do it better, or at least as well as the people who were speaking and teaching. When I did leave my former job, and I saw that I could make enough money doing this, it made it all seem worthwhile! I worked that much harder with a stronger motivation. That was my tipping point, just seeing my potential in full force. I was also encouraged by having a senior executive at my former company tell me to just go out and follow my bliss.

Q: What is your motivation now that you have success?

A: The drive for me is in seeing and hearing when people finally "get it" with topics in IT. My job is not necessarily to write straight technical, knowledge-based articles, but to translate complex topics into terms that people can understand. When I get that feeling that I've really connected with a magazine reader or a conference attendee, it brings a real sense of fulfillment for my work.

Q: What would you say was one of your biggest challenges?

A: For me, one of the biggest challenges was just making the jump and learning to trust in myself. When you work for yourself, you make all the decisions, and when you make a wrong one, you have to live with it. You are stuck with doing it. It's a whole new level of accountability! It's your reputation on the line and you must deal directly with the consequences.

Q: What has been the best or most unexpected reward for you?

A: Getting to work with the community I admire, and being in that inner circle of people I admired and looked up to. Being considered a peer now, by those who I once looked up to, is very rewarding.

Q: Any thoughts on how to attract, retain, and motivate em-

CONCENTRATED TECHNOLOGY

ployees? What is the most important attribute you look for? Thoughts on the employee-ownership model?

A: I have always loved the saying, "Work today, pay today." I like the self empowering aspect and money is good! The key for me, is having a direct linkage between effort and reward. What I mean by that is to get paid for a result and to be in control of one's earnings. A salary provides no incentive to excel. I don't think anyone should ever be salaried. Doing so discourages change, team-work, and excelling. It just encourages mediocrity. You get paid regardless of the result. You need to give employees real incentives and eliminate the hourly constraints that an 8-5 job creates. You should give the worker complete flexibility. In my world, an extra week of vacation would be preferred over a raise. I don't ever intend on having any employees, because some of the happiest people I know are companies of one. Smaller is better. That way, teams can know each other by their first names. People are more willing and able to perform better in smaller teams, this drives a great level of empowerment and an overall higher level of respect. All of this becomes impossible when a company grows big.

> *"People are more willing and able to perform better in smaller teams, this drives a great level of empowerment and an overall higher level of respect."*

Q: Is there a book you would recommend for an entrepreneur in the making?

A: *The Ropes to Skip and the Ropes to Know: Studies in Organizational Behavior* by R. Richard Ritti and Steven Levy.

Q: What do you attribute your success to? What core beliefs or values have helped you persevere?

A: Well, I have developed four rules for success that I always detail to others who seek me out for advice. This is a model I have followed for most of my life...

GREG SHIELDS

CONCENTRATED TECHNOLOGY

GREG SHIELDS' FOUR RULES FOR SUCCESS

1. You don't have to do something that is new or different, in fact it's harder when you do because you have to convince others that it makes sense in the first place.

2. Always be on time. When you agree to do something, do it and do it by when you said you would.

3. Do good work. You don't always have to do great work. People aren't paying for 'great work', they just want to get it done. Perfectionism can kill you.

4. Rule number 2 is more important than rule number 3. If you do good work, people will come back, but if you don't deliver and let people down, then your credibility will be called into question and then it is very hard to regain their trust.

Q: If there was one slogan that you base your life on, or perhaps the quote that you'd want on your tombstone, what would it be?

A: When in doubt, go higher.

49

"Get up to bat and take a swing."
Greg Stroh, mix1

◆

BACKGROUND
You name it and Greg Stroh has been there, done that. Greg Stroh worked for his family's company Stroh Brewery Co. for eleven years. He is the cofounder of the IZZE Beverage Co. Now, Greg Stroh brings us mix1, an all-natural "functional beverage" as one of three cofounders.

INTERVIEW
Q: What was your initial startup cost and the source?
A: $1.8 million, angels investors.

Q: How long until you reached a positive cash flow?
A: We are projecting profit within four to five years. Everything we make, we put right back into marketing and sales. For us, it's all about gaining market share right now.

Q: Did you use a business plan?
A: Yes, and we have changed it significantly at least two to three times.

Q: What was the genesis of the idea?
A: I knew Dr. James Rouse from my days at IZZE. We were always throwing around ideas back then. I met him for lunch one day and we were discussing how his patients were always asking for an all-natural meal replacement, and none existed! Ensure and Boost were the only ones in the market doing at least $500 million a year, and they are both owned by large pharmaceutical companies.

Q: What is the vision of the company and the community you serve? What came first, the problem or the solution?
A: The problem existed, and we wanted to create a true func-

tional beverage to serve the market. We envisioned creating the highest quality all-natural products, to have a truly functional nutrition for wellness and peak performance that promotes health, wellness, and performance. Our passion is to define the functional beverage market.

Q: What is the passion that it fills for you personally?
A: To create something from nothing. Putting it all on the line and taking risks. Free enterprise is something unique to the US as compared to most other countries. I feel I have an obligation to embrace it. I enjoy wearing all the different hats it takes to run a company; it's fun!

> *"It's important not to second guess yourself, or dwell on the mistakes but to learn from them and move on quickly."*

Q: Where do you see yourself and your company in 10 years?
A: Having an international presence, to be the product that has defined a new functional beverage market. To have expanded products beyond the mix1 drinks we have today.

Q: What are the biggest challenges as an entrepreneur in general?
A: It's easy to be the Monday morning quarterback and see all the faults in everything going wrong around you. You need to have a thick skin and be willing to wear multiple hats. As an entrepreneur, you will make mistakes. The big question will be how do you deal with your mistakes and stick together as a team. Will you be able to react quickly? You have to focus on the problem, not the person. It's important not to second guess yourself or dwell on the mistakes but to learn from them and move on quickly. Your success will be defined by how well you react to challenges and adversity. The best advice I can give is that you just have to be willing to step up to the plate and take a swing.

Q: What aspects of ownership are the most rewarding?
A: The positive feedback I get and the pride in seeing our product out there. I love watching people we hire blossom and

MIX1

realize their full potential and accomplish the success that results from their efforts.

Q: Are there one or two things you can attribute your success to? Luck, timing, someone who helped you?

A: I am grateful for my partners, Dr. James Rouse and Brasher, and a wonderful team I work with at mix1. The key to any winning team is having great teammates!

Q: What is the most important attribute you look for in an employee?

A: The first and foremost important thing they must have is passion. They must have passion for the product, the company, and the idea. Everyone here is passionate about nutrition. I seek people who have an entrepreneurial mindset, that is, willing to take risks and be innovative and never settling for the status quo.

Q: Do you recommend any books or possibly an MBA?

A: I don't have an MBA myself but I think it is valuable to hire MBAs. There are many books I could recommend, but the ones that are on the top of my mind right now are *The Tipping Point* by Malcom Gladwell and *Purple Cow* by Seth Godin.

Q: Slogan to live by or what it might say on your tombstone?

A: "Get up to bat and take a swing, just go for it!" and "Believe in yourself, you'll be a lot more fun to be around." There is a fine line in not being conceded, but you do need to love yourself and know you have a lot to offer the world. It starts with believing in yourself!

Q: Is there anything else you'd like to share?

A: I think the worst thing you can do is get overly focused on the end point of where you think your company will be, it distracts you and you will wind up missing other opportunities. Mid-stage, you just want to create options. If you're having fun and enjoy-

> *"Believe in yourself, you'll be a lot more fun to be around."*

GREG STROH

235

ing yourself, success will happen, but if you are in it for the end game, others will sense it and you won't attract the right people or success. Be sure you know the main drivers of your business. In our model, it's all about sales and marketing. We outsource everything except for sales and marketing because we know that's what it takes to be successful. I think back to the many microbreweries that were good but went out of business in the 90's. If you look at the ones that failed, you'll see that they tried to do it all. The successful ones like Sam Adams focused on the sales and marketing, knowing that finding and pleasing customers was the most important thing.

GREG'S TIPS FROM THE TRENCHES

1. Don't overstress the goal of where you want to take your company or you will miss things along the way.

2. Have fun!

3. Know your key business drivers.

4. Outsource what you can.

MIX1

50

"You can't learn to swim if you are hanging on the side of the pool."

Jon Susa, Susa Insurance Agency

◆

BACKGROUND

Jon Susa, is an independent insurance agent for Farmers Group. He started the Susa Insurance Agency in 2006. His office is located in Fort Collins, Colorado and he currently has one employee. Jon's startup cost was $5,000 with no outside funding. He had no previous entrepreneurial experience. Jon had worked as a bartender for 15 years when he finally made the jump into the entrepreneurial world.

INTERVIEW

Q: What was the genesis of the idea?

A: It was a conversation with a friend who ran a job placement company. The question that sparked the desire was "What do you want to get out of your job?". In other words, you need to first look at what you need to get out of your job, and then look for a career that can fulfill that need. I was literally recruited into Farmers Group by the area manager who saw that I possessed excellent customer service skills, something I feel you either have or you don't – it is a skill that can't be taught.

Q: How long did it take you until your business earned a positive cash flow?

A: About two years. I stayed at my former job until I had built up enough clients to make the leap to pursuing my business full-time. I cut my hours back to 20 hours a week as a bartender and worked 40 hours a week building my insurance practice.

Q: Did you use a business plan?

A: I did.

Q: Have you had to modify it to meet the demands of the market?

A: Yes, I update it about once a year.

Q: Where do you see yourself and your company in 10 years?

A: I see my agency having six to 10 employees, doing the tasks that I don't enjoy. That will give me more time to focus on building relationships with my clients and it will allow me more time to spend on marketing and promotions.

> *"...first look at what you need to get out of your job, and then look for a career that can fulfill that need."*

Q: What is the passion that it fills for you personally?

A: Personal relationships. Being an insurance agent allows me to connect at a deeper level with others.

Q: What were your biggest challenges? What do you know now that you wish you had known sooner?

A: Convincing people early on that you are in it for the long haul was the biggest challenge for me. When people pick an insurance agent they want someone who'll be there for them when the need arises. Early on, I could have utilized better time management. What I mean by that is being productive versus busy. I found that for the first six months, I was very busy, but not necessarily productive. My philosophy is that in my business, you should treat your office like a boat: you only spend 20% of your time actually in it!

Q: What were your biggest rewards? What aspects of ownership are the most rewarding? Have you found any unexpected rewards?

A: The transferability of the skills as a bartender to being a good agent. It's all about customer service. My client base with my bartending job dovetailed nicely into my prospect base for my insurance business. The switch from working nights to working days was a great bonus.

Q: Are there one or two things you can attribute your success

Susa Insurance Agency

to?

A: Being like a chameleon, that is, being able to leave my personal beliefs and opinions at the door. Getting along with anyone and listening to what is most important to them. I also had a strong desire to become an expert in this field in order to help my clients. I have always viewed myself as self-employed which I believe has also helped encourage me to get to this point in my life.

Q: Strongest core beliefs?

A: That you are always on duty. In other words, you are always maintaining high integrity and a strong work ethic, even outside of work.

Q: How do you attract and retain the best employees? What is the most important attribute you look for?

A: You can find excellent employees in any industry – you just need to look for superior customer service oriented people. I am proof that it is one of the most vital transferable skills. I believe bonuses are an ideal method to motivate employees to stay with their company and work harder.

Q: Do you recommend any books, resources or an MBA?

A: My wife got her MBA and I felt that it was highly beneficial for her. I was even able to pick up a few tips from her along the way. For books, I would recommend Michael E. Gerber's *The E-Myth: Why Most Businesses Don't Work and What to Do About It* and *The Millionaire Next Door* by Thomas J. Stanley and William D. Danko.

> *"I have always viewed myself as self-employed which I believe has also helped encourage me to get to this point in my life."*

Q: Slogan to live by or what it might say on your tombstone?

A: "You can't learn to swim if you are hanging on the side of the pool." If you are not having fun, go find something else to do!

"The secret to true contentment lies not in trying to satisfy every craving or desire, but in learning to be satisfied with all the things you have. That is the reality of sharing the world with others."

- Tadahiko Nagao

51

"No pleasure in idleness."

April Thayer, Hubbuzz.com

◆

BACKGROUND

Founded in Centennial, Colorado in 2007, *Hubbuzz.com* is the fourth startup for April Thayer. After spending fifteen years at the helm of Thayer Media, April and her team of six employees are now focused on building Hubbuzz into the most innovative and preferred apartment search site on the web.

INTERVIEW

Q: What was your initial startup cost and source of funding?

A: We've invested over $750,000 so far and tapped approximately $750,000 in soft money-assets and office space from Thayer Media.

Q: How long until there was a positive cash flow?

A: We're projecting positive cash flow by March 2009.

Q: Did you use a business plan? If so, did you have to modify the original business plan to meet the demands of the market?

A: No, I am letting "proforma" drive our business and am closely monitoring metrics and making adjustments as needed.

Q: What came first, the problem or the solution?

A: The problem came first. I noticed there wasn't any good apartment/resident location services that searched by community. The tools I found didn't appeal to the Gen Y youth graduating from college.

Q: What is the passion that it fills for you personally?

A: The whole process of setting a goal and achieving it feeds my competitive spirit. I enjoy building something out of nothing and enjoy the constant challenges and continual learning.

APRIL THAYER

Q: What was the genesis of the idea?

A: The first time I went into business one of my friends said, "You know how to do this April. You should start your own business". I also read a lot. One article I read was about how Gen X and Gen Y use the web and how different their world is than the one I grew up in. The article mentioned the need of the younger generation to be part of a community and the mention of neighborhoods in the article was the catalyst of the idea.

Q: Where do you see yourself and your company in 10 years?

A: For the company to have significant profits within five years and to see it off within ten years so I can semi-retire and try something else. *Rent.com* is currently earning $9 million per month with only 150 employees!

Q: Biggest challenges? What do you know now that you wish you'd known sooner?

A: We would have spent more time on market research/intelligence regarding the markets we went after. Certain markets are a better fit for Hubbuzz than others. Spending time on a market that was not a good fit has set us back a bit. Raising money has been more time consuming and more difficult than I envisioned. I wish I had begun fundraising on day one. Talking to people who had done it before and getting some coaching would have been helpful. The concept of raising money is new to me because I've always gone the 'bootstrap' path with my former companies.

> *"...time has taught me that confidence in yourself and others is the key ingredient; things will work out even though you may not be able to see how or why."*

Q: What is your biggest reward? What aspects of ownership are the most rewarding?

A: The sense of shared ownership that I've created something bigger than myself and the six person team. We all feel a sense of being part of something big and exciting. The international press I've received has been an unexpected reward.

HUBBUZZ.COM

The ongoing positive feedback I receive from my clients is fulfilling and confirms that we have something special in the market.

Q: Are there one or two things you can attribute your success to? Was it luck, timing, someone who helped you, etc.?

A: My mom inspired me. She instilled a strong work and a never ending self-improvement philosophy in myself and my siblings. My mom is Icelandic and has a Viking's drive. She is always busy and never stops learning and trying new things. She taught me if you work hard you will be rewarded for your efforts. I attribute my success to always looking one step ahead (sometimes being on the bleeding edge), a willingness to always try new things, and a team that supports me and all my crazy ideas. I've also found that you always need to be one step ahead of your clients and asking yourself what's the next question you can be asking them to continue expanding your value to them. At one point in my life as an entrepreneur I told myself, I'll never go into business for myself again. However time has taught me that confidence in yourself and others is the key ingredient; things will work out even though you may not be able to see how or why.

Q: How do you attract and retain the best employees? What is the most important attribute you look for?

A: I hand-picked my current staff from my former company, Thayer Media. My staff is process-oriented and follows a proven method for success. The best employees are explorers and are process-driven. They possess a younger mindset and are web savvy. They also have a strong work ethic and are willing to do whatever it takes, even if it sometimes means working late and on weekends.

Q: Can you recommend any training or resources such as books, classes, or websites? Do you recommend an MBA?

A: No on the MBA. I don't even feel a college degree is necessary to be an entrepreneur. What is important is getting out on the field and playing full out and learning from your mistakes. You find the best solutions by working through problems and you learn the most in those moments. For books I'd

APRIL THAYER

recommend, *What Clients Love: A Field Guild to Growing Your Business* by Harry Beckwith, *Under the Radar: Talking to Today's Cynical Consumer* by Jonathan Bond, and *E-Myth* by Michael Gerber. I'm currently reading *Punk Marketing* by Richard Laermer.

> *"What is important is getting out on the field and playing full out and learning from your mistakes."*

Q: What is your slogan to live by or what might it say on your tombstone?

A: "No pleasure in idleness". Work drives me; it's the most important aspect of my day. I view work as fun, especially hard work.

"She wasn't afraid to think big"
Donna Visocky, BellaSpark Productions

◆

BACKGROUND

Donna Visocky founded BellaSpark Productions in 2002. With its current five employees, BellaSpark Productions offers motivational workshops, seminars, events, and even produces a free publication for the holistic community, *The Healing Path*. Donna's past entrepreneurial experiences include owning a cheese and gift shop and a direct mail business. Donna was also a partner of a skating apparel company. Her initial startup cost was $50,000, obtained via a second mortgage and credit cards.

INTERVIEW

Q: How long did it take you until your business earned a positive cash flow?

A: About one year.

Q: Did you use a business plan?

A: Not really, but I did use an outline.

Q: What was the genesis of the idea?

A: I was led to start my business after my 21 year old daughter Kristi died in a car accident. Her death opened me up to a new level of spirituality, which brought me to read and study the works of many of the top metaphysical and spiritual teachers of our time. Having been an organizer and event planner for years, I felt compelled to use my experience and skills to share this information with others. Many people, myself included, are looking for answers, trying to make sense out of life. I want to provide people with an opportunity to explore different concepts and perhaps help them on their own spiritual journey. I brought in one speaker as a test and was surprised by the response from the community; the business has taken off from there.

DONNA VISOCKY

Q: What is the vision of your company and the community you serve?

A: Bella means beautiful and Spark reflects how my daughter Kristi was in life. Kristi was the catalyst behind BellaSpark and the company exists today as a tribute to her ongoing legacy. Our tag line is "igniting change" and our mission is to be a spark that exposes every day ordinary people to extraordinary new thoughts in order to inspire a more spiritually-conscious way of living. BellaSpark brings powerful, thought-provoking speakers to people around the country. Our free publication, *The Healing Path*, serves the market of those seeking positive reinforcement and deeper spiritual lives.

> *"I feel the hunger in people as they search for answers to the meaning of life; I have that same hunger."*

Q: What is the passion that your business fills for you personally?

A: I feel the hunger in people as they search for answers to the meaning of life; I have that same hunger. I am passionate about helping to fill that yearning with inspiring information. To be able to help people find their own answers, to open them up to new ideas, that is my purpose.

Q: Where do you see yourself and your company in 10 years?

A: I'd like to franchise the magazine to new markets and create multiple city tours for my speakers. I envision taking BellaSpark to greater heights. I see exciting and unique things for the company.

Q: What were your biggest challenges? Looking back now, is there anything you wish you had done differently? Any regrets?

A: I wish I had spent more time building up systems, so that I was better able to delegate my duties to others. I know how to do everything myself, but I never make the time to train someone else. Having better systems would allow me to focus more on the big picture and allow others to provide the details. My only regret is that I wish I would have started

BellaSpark Productions

BellaSpark sooner!

Q: What have been your biggest rewards? What aspects of ownership are the most rewarding?

A: An awareness that there is nothing to be afraid of in life. The direct appreciation I get from others. The freedom. The people I have met and the deep connection with others, has been an unexpected reward. Being able to expand my business to a place I love, Seattle. I would also say the sense of peace that comes from only having to please yourself has been so satisfying!

> *"Having better systems would allow me to focus more on the big picture and allow others to provide the details."*

Q: Are there one or two things you can attribute your success to? Luck, timing, someone who helped you along the way?

A: I believe everything has gone according to a plan bigger than myself. I'm simply fulfilling on a plan already laid out. Kristi's death really woke me up. I attribute my success to perseverance and having a good support group of fellow business owners.

Q: How do you attract and retain the best employees? What is the most important attribute you look for?

A: The most important thing is that a person has to have a passion for whatever "it" is. The best thing you can find in a prospective employee is genuine enthusiasm and passion.

Q: Any recommended training and resources? Do you recommend an MBA?

A: Any book that helps you stick with your passion is worth the read. A good one is *The Answer* by John Assaroff. As for an MBA, I'm not sure because I don't have one. My advice is to spend effort on anything that helps ignite the passion within.

Q: Slogan to live by or what it might say on your tombstone?

A: "She wasn't afraid to think big."

DONNA VISOCKY

"The clock of life is wound but once,
And no man has the power to tell
just when the hands will stop at late
or early hour. To lose one's wealth is
sad indeed. Too lose one's health is
more. To lose one's soul is such a loss
that no man can restore. Today, only
is our own. So live, love and toil with
a will. Place no faith in tommorrow,
For the clock may soon be still."

- Robert H Smith

"He went for everything."
David Wood, Solution Box

◆

BACKGROUND

David Wood started Solution Box in 1998. He doesn't have a permanent address. He spends time all over the world, and runs a highly successful, thriving business in cyberspace. He's written several ebooks and is currently writing what will be his first professionally published work titled, *The Wealthy Gypsy*. David is the kind of personality Tim Ferriss described in *The 4 Hour Work Week*; only David had been living that way long before *The 4-Hour Work Week* was ever published. It was Tim Ferriss that inspired David to write *The Wealthy Gypsy*. David currently works with approximately five contractors and works in the training, life coaching, and internet marketing field. Solution Box was his first real venture, although he did spend a year traveling the world as a one-man band. He offers several free valuable ebooks on the topic of life coaching on his website at *www.solutionbox.com*.

INTERVIEW

Q: What was your initial startup cost and source of funding?

A: $35 to cover the cost of an hour with a coach and business cards.

Q: Did you use a business plan? Have you had to morph your original business plan to meet the demands of the market?

A: No, namely because I wasn't originally seeking any capital. Any time I have written business plans, they tend to look more like marketing plans anyway.

Q: What was the genesis of the idea?

A: The idea began after I took the Landmark Education forum. I was coaching people in those courses and it became what I

DAVID WOOD

enjoyed most. I was surprised to learn you could make a living doing it, but realized you could when someone handed me a business card that said "Coach." I learned the business from the first two coaches I hired (David Griffiths and Christine McDougall). For the first few years, I was coaching others and just sending out a newsletter now and then. Things began to take off when I applied to speak at the first annual Australian Coaches Conference. I got the gig and had to come up with a compelling talk. The title of my speech was "How to Get Your First 50 Clients." I negotiated to retain all the rights to the speech and was able to offer it as my first product after it was recorded. I put the audio download on my website and sold it for $39.00. Would you believe I sold that recording over 4,000 times? Since then, I've learned the value of creating (and owning) your own content.

> *"I don't believe in regret... there's no way of knowing how things would have worked out had you made different decisions along the way."*

SOLUTION BOX

Q: What is the vision of the company and the community you serve?

A: I help people achieve their goals and love their life. What really lights me up is to help people generate the courage they need to live an extraordinary life. My community is anyone with a goal! Initially, it was anyone willing to invest in making real changes in themselves. I've carved out a niche coaching other coaches with an emphasis on internet marketing. I help people who want to make a living from coaching, and give them the ability to expand their niche and teach others to do the same. Coaching is a wonderful lifestyle, it gives you the freedom to work whenever and wherever you want to!

Q: What is the passion that it fills for you personally?

A: Seeing others express themselves fully. I truly have a passion for business – particularly the marketing and branding aspects of it. I love the process of creating new systems, new content, and figuring out how to automate it.

Q: Where do you see yourself and your company in 10 years?

A: Having a string of best-selling books on personal growth and business issues, then up-selling to bigger ticket backend products. Being involved in a television show and perhaps a radio show. A network of contractors managing many of my projects for profit share, and some sort of charity involvement.

Q: What were your biggest challenges? Looking back, is there anything you wish you had done differently?

A: I don't believe in regret, it's a way of torturing yourself. There's no way of knowing how things would have worked out had you made different decisions along the way. However, I have learned how powerful it is to

> *"I've always believed the best way to learn how to do something right is to talk to people doing it successfully."*

pick a niche and focus your efforts on a single market. John Gray did it with *Men are from Mars, Women are from Venus*. You want to build a powerful brand like that, associate it with your name, and in doing so you will inevitable be pulled into other niches. Having a book is great for credibility. It's the most powerful business card you can have. But in most cases, you can't make a living from book sales alone. The key is leveraging that book to open the door to other streams of income.

Q: What were your biggest rewards? What aspects of ownership are the most rewarding?

A: I have total control over what I do and when I do it with no restrictions. I'm not imprisoned like I was when I worked in corporate America. Total freedom for me is demonstrated by the fact that I left New York this past July, and headed for Australia to see my brother. It's November and I'm still here, by choice.

Q: Are there one or two things you can attribute your success to? Was it luck, timing, someone who helped you, etc.?

A: I've always believed the best way to learn how to do some-

DAVID WOOD

thing right is to talk to people doing it successfully. Whatever "it" is, ask them how they got there. Tony Fitzgerald and Max Hitchens are two such people whom I approached for help. This made a big difference when I started out. Just go talk to successful people. Not all of them are going to offer help, but many of them will open doors for you. I'm always trying new things. I'm always curious. It's important not to under-estimate the hard work needed in the beginning. It's going to very hard work early on, and you have to keep your focus and persistence, always trying new things. You will fail more than you succeed, and that's why you have to try so many different things. I have learned that joint ventures can work well. Pay-per-click used to work, but less so today. You have to always be asking yourself, "What's next?"

Q: How do you attract and retain the best employees? What is the most important attribute you look for?

A: I'll admit this is not my strength. I've been more of a "solo-preneur." In spite of that, I've managed to grow my business. My mailing list has been the best hiring tool I have. I send out a request of what I'm looking for to my list of 70,000 people, and I then get back responses. The beauty of our model is that it doesn't matter where they live. And best of all, I get to work with people who already know me. Beth Dargis, who has been my assistant for five years, is a glowing example, and she has been such a key player in the journey.

Q: What training and resources do you recommend? Do you recommend an MBA?

A: No on the MBA. I highly recommend people visit *Solution-box.com* as well as Landmark Education. The books I suggest are *E-Myth* by Michael Gerber and *The 4-Hour Work Week* by Tim Ferris.

Q: What is your slogan to live by or what it might say on your tombstone?

A: "He went for everything."

EPILOGUE

As a conclusion to *50 Interviews: Entrepreneurs*, I thought it fitting to have myself interviewed. This final interview was performed by my good friend, Carrie Pinsky of Pink Sky Writing.

"There are certain things you can only understand by creating them yourself."
Brian Schwartz, 50 Interviews Inc.™

◆

BACKGROUND

What began as a career experiment actually became Brian's new career. He started 50 Interviews Inc.™ after he began interviewing fifty entrepreneurs across all industries. In the process, Brian got in touch with the entrepreneur within. He became convinced that the interview process held widespread potential to teach and inspire others on their own particular journeys. He quit his stressful fifty hour a week job, took a less demanding job and is now spending more time fulfilling his passion, and the vision of *50 Interviews™*.

INTERVIEW

Q: Do you have positive cash flow?

A: Not yet. I expect positive cash flow within the first year. I have already invested at least $5,000, and will probably invest another $5,000-$10,000 in the next 6 months.

Q: Do you have a business plan?

A: No.

Q: What was the genesis of the idea?

A: My wife, Debi, knew I was exploring the idea of leaving my steady job to start my own business. She suggested that I talk to other people who had taken similar risks to strike out on their own. As a matter of fact, she told me to talk to 50 people. She'll admit today that she never thought I would make it through 50 interviews. She figured I would get tired of meeting with people and give up the idea of working for myself. It was an agreement between us that I would not take action until I had done 50 interviews. Normally, I tend to get bored and my passion for an idea will peter out. This time my wife's plan backfired. So, I owe it all to my wife. She was the catalyst for the idea.

> *"There is no self-doubt that it is the right thing for me to be doing. "*

Q: What came first, the problem or the solution?

A: The problem. I kept waking up at night and wondering why I was unfulfilled in my life. I was approaching my 40th birthday and wondering, "Is this all there is?" It was, in many ways, a classic mid-life crisis. You begin to see that your life is not going to last forever and that money is not the key to happiness.

Q: What is the vision of the company and the community you serve?

A: The community that this book serves is anyone who has ever had an idea, but has not taken action on it. The ultimate goal is to inspire action. I hope others will read *50 Interviews™* and see the evidence they need to know what is possible. That others use this as a framework to discover a truth for themselves.

Q: Is there a passion this fills for you personally?

A: When I am working on this project, there is no self-doubt that it is the right thing for me to be doing. I feel that others are being impacted by the project, and their enthusiasm is helping fuel the idea. For years, I enjoyed doing triathlons. One of my favorite events was called "Escape from Alcatraz." They take you out on a boat about a mile from shore. You jump into the icy waters and you swim to the shore. There is no option. I see this similar to being an entrepreneur. Once you step off the ledge, there is no option but to make it happen. You will figure out a way to succeed or you will learn valuable lessons in the process. Either way, there is no choice but to keep going. That is how I feel now that I have committed to becoming an entrepreneur. There is no turning back. Tom Frey, one of the interviewees articulates this well when he told me, "Once the wiring has changed, there is no going back."

Q: Where do you see yourself and your company in 10 years?

A: This is my full time job. Traveling around the world speaking about this project, writing and inspiring others to use the framework as a means to ultimately find more fulfillment in their life as I have. I hope I won't know where Friday ends and Monday begins because the weekends will be just as fulfilling for me as Monday through Friday. Within 10 years, I hope to be a sought after speaker who is rewarded for the value I bring to others. I want everyone who authors books in this series to have the same opportunities.

Q: What are the biggest challenges you have faced thus far? Looking back, is there anything you wish you had done differently?

A: This is a tough question because I am still evolving. I wish I would have stayed on top of writing and editing the interviews as I went along. I wish I had committed time to the process everyday. At the time, I did not realize that the interviews themselves were going to spark my business idea. Maybe this question should not be included in any of the

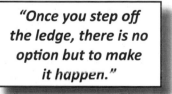

"Once you step off the ledge, there is no option but to make it happen."

interviews because most every entrepreneur that I spoke to seemed to live without regret. It's not in the entrepreneur's make up to spend time looking in the rear view mirror wishing things had been different.

Q: Biggest rewards? What aspects of ownership are the most rewarding?

A: Through the process of doing the interviews and starting my business I have extended my circle and developed my relationships with others. I have really begun to see the world through eyes of abundance rather than scarcity. I used to envy certain people or feel pangs of jealousy towards others. I no longer feel that way. I see others as peers who have struggled just the same as I have. The process of talking to people has leveled the playing field, and I now see that we all battle similar issues. One of the most unexpected rewards has been the sense of fulfillment that I am finding. I did not know this level of fulfillment was even accessible to me. The high I get from the work I am doing is similar to the endorphin high I used to experience when competing in triathlons. Being able to access that at any time is amazing.

> *"It's not in the entrepreneur's make up to spend time looking in the rear view mirror wishing things had been different."*

Q: Are there one or two things you can attribute your success to? Luck, timing, someone who helped you along the way?

A: First of all, Landmark Education. I attribute Landmark for helping me with the process of self-discovery as well as getting the project off the ground. Rob McNealy from *Start Up Radio* in Denver really took me under his wing, and made some amazing introductions for me. I credit a lot of my success to his willingness to help me get started. Veronica Yager has been working tirelessly to edit and format the book. She is a talented force and a very tenacious worker. She has an amazing work ethic. I think that it is important to surround yourself with people who believe in you and who bring complimentary skills to the table.

> *"I have really begun to see the world through eyes of abundance, rather than scarcity."*

Q: How do you attract and retain the best employees? What is the most important quality you look for?

A: I share my passion with others. About 1 out of 100 people seem inclined to take some initiative in the project. I share

50 INTERVIEWS INC.™

my vision and look for others who can see the bigger picture. It's also about people who believe in me. One thing that Landmark taught me was to hang out with people who see my possibilities rather than my limitations. Many of us are surrounded by people who fail to see our possibilities because they identify with us as our past. And who we are should not be defined by our past, but the future we choose to live into. Human beings grow and discover new things. I think it is important for people to be open to the fact that people change.

Q: Anything else you would like to add?

A: There are certain things you can only understand by creating them yourself. The moment you have an inspired thought, take action on it and start creating it for yourself. If you are inspired to do something... just do one thing towards making it happen and it will become real. Also, there is a skill in listening. I am often reminded of this myself. Stop talking and listen for a while. It's hard to do. So, no matter how much you think you know, be open to constructive criticism and be open to the reality of someone else's mindset. When you separate yourself from your ego, you can use the feedback and information to improve your life. Other people's perceptions about life can offer you amazing insights into your own experience. Reading *50 Interviews*™ can help others, but the bigger hope is that people will clue into the power that comes from listening and learning from others to gain valuable insights and inspiration.

> *"Who we are is not defined by our past but the future we choose to live into."*

BRIAN SCHWARTZ

Carrie Pinsky's Bio:
Carrie Pinsky is a freelance writer, facilitator and collaborator. Her background is in human resources and organizational development. Whether Carrie is writing, recruiting or conducting interactive workshops, she strives to provide ideas and information to help individuals and organizations achieve higher levels of success.
www.PinkSkyWriting.com

"Time has no value in death."

- Debi J. Schwartz

APPENDIX A

A Life Driven By Values

By Ken Munsch, President, Cattleman's Choice Loomix, LLC
www.loomix.com

Look for mentors in your personal and professional life. In my life I have had five mentors that allowed me to establish the value system that drives me, and ultimately led to my success. My first mentor was my mother. She taught me to respect people and have faith in them. My second mentor was my wife, Dolly. She taught me never to waste a day being upset because we will never get that day back. My third mentor was my first boss, Dave Stornetta. He taught me the right thing to do is to tell everyone I love, how much I love them everyday, and to live a balanced life. My fourth mentor was my first corporate boss, Mike Reed. He taught me the "bottom line" rule in business and how to keep it positive. My last mentor is my current business partner, Mike Troska. Mike taught me the way a partnership works is through brutal honesty, trust, and communications.

These mentors helped me to establish my values early in life. I live my values and my values are what drives me. My entire business life I have been driven by these basic core values. At the core of my values are my faith and my family. I can't separate the two. They are both number one in my life. Nothing separates them. Neither is first and neither is second. The third thing in my life is my "job". Nothing will ever come before my faith/family, including my job. After that, nothing will ever come before my job. No hobby, no night on the town, no Rotary Club, nothing will ever come before my job with the exception of my faith and my family.

To follow through with these values, you must first be very disciplined and steadfast in finding your passion. And secondly, you must find a "job" that accepts the value of your family and your faith within your life. Not so hard. Most of my principles are my own, but in a couple of places I borrowed great wisdom that was already out there. The following are the ten values that I live by and what drives me:

1. **Express your love:** Don't be afraid to tell someone you love them. If you love someone why not share that with them? Don't say it in passing, say it from the heart. They will know if it is heartfelt. This includes your family, your parents, and your siblings and in my case the "extended Loomix company family". End every telephone call with your family by sharing with them that you love them and how much you appreciate them. When speaking at conventions and business meetings I tell people to make sure to tell their loved ones that they love them. Every time I am finished speaking someone comes up to me with tears in their eyes thanking me for getting them "over the hump" and ready to go home and tell someone they love them.

2. **Get your immediate family involved so they can buy into your business:** Look for ways to get your family involved in your business. Sometimes it is simple things like bringing clients to your home for a meal or attending company outings. For example, on birthdays, consider inviting your business associates' family over as well. The more you look for opportunities, the more you will find. My mother stills wears an old company jacket that I gave her and my Grandfather wore our company winter cap that I gave him every time it would get cold out for years. My mom has been to our national dealer meeting (prior to me being an owner) and my mom, brother, and all my children, have been on company incentive trips. Even if they are not involved in the business, my immediate family attends national company functions to enjoy time with their extended "Loomix family".

3. **Make your staff/customers your "extended family," and do it from the heart:** Our company is national in scope and this has made our "extended Loomix family" very large and quite diverse. We want our staff/customers to make their entire family part of our "extended Loomix family". Parents and children are invited to our national meetings. This year our incentive winners were invited to bring their entire family to Walt Disney World. We send new members of our ex-

tended family a Loomix jacket and overalls when they are born. We share in their proud moments and their moments of pain. My wife and children know the families of most of our staff/customers and our staff/customers ask about them often. My family loves their "adopted Loomix family" and we are sure that love is reciprocated. During my very recent bout with cancer, I was deluged with prayers, cards, letters, and emails from both of my families and the word love was mentioned often.

4. **Listen and respond to your spouse:** My biggest and boldest move in my business life was when I gave up my career after spending nearly twenty years going from the bottom of the company to the top. My wife sacrificed and moved our family eight different times. It was about the time I reached the top when my wife suffered a stroke. She spent six months in the hospital and over the next three years, I helped her through rehabilitation. In the middle of her rehab she told me that she would love to move back to Colorado, one of our stops in my career path. That is the first time she ever asked me for something of this magnitude in my entire career. So, I found a way to get the company I was working for to sell me and my partner a piece of the business I was working in and move it to Colorado. Our business has enjoyed great growth in the past twelve years, making a profit every year. My wife kept her personal dream alive while I reached even higher levels of fulfillment.

5. **Free time is family time:** All of my free time my entire married life has been spent with my family. Today I sit on a number of boards and committees on a national level. My wife attends every meeting with me, many times being the only spouse there. They are always happy to include her in many of the "fun" activities. She spends the rest of the time shopping. At night when I come home, we walk for an hour discussing the day, have a drink and dinner. When she goes to bed I often go to work at home. I followed the same pattern raising my children. My son, Preston and I have been to nearly every major league football and baseball team and hundreds of college sporting events together. My wife

and I traveled all over the country with our oldest daughter, Heather, while she competed in twirling and modeling while she was growing up. I made a special point to be there when my youngest daughter, Sheena who was a preemie, was born. I made sure I was there to help get her through those first critical stages, all while advancing in my career. I attended nearly every one of my children's school functions and parent teacher conferences. When I hear that old saying, "where there is a will there is a way," I like to add, "to have your way, you must have the will".

6. **The power of prayer:** A couple of months ago I was diagnosed with a very aggressive type of prostate cancer. My wife and three children had never seen me in such a weakened position. They were experiencing something they had never before witnessed. A few nights after my diagnosis, my wife and I were at a hockey game. We have five great seats on the glass next to our team's bench. When we don't have any friends with us, we often go up into the stands and pick out someone who we think will enjoy sitting in these great seats. That night we picked out a gentleman and his son. During the game we started to really enjoy our time with them. We introduced ourselves and asked the gentleman what he did. It turned out the gentleman was Darin Gleghorn, the pastor of the Northern Colorado Cowboy Church. Later in the game I told him about my cancer and he asked if he could pray for me. He prayed right there on the spot. He prayed for me to be healed, but also for the great wisdom of my surgeon. A few days later I had my surgery and then found out the results of my lab samples. The assisting surgeon gave us the good news. His first words were "thank goodness your surgeon had great wisdom". You see, we all had hoped that the cancer was confined to the prostate but it wasn't. The surgeon took a wider margin at just the right place and my cancer was removed with negative margins. I know many would say this was a coincidence. But in my life I have seen so many "coincidences".

7. **Make the leap from good to great:** In Jim Collin's best selling book *Good to Great* he refers to those people who can make

the leap from good to great. He said they all are deeply passionate about what they do, they know they can be the best in the world at what they do, and they are compensated enough to drive their economic engine. After reading this on an airplane one day, I came home and gathered all of our staff together to ask them one question; "Who is the best liquid feed company in the world?" Going around the room from our technical department, sales, accounting, customer service, and production staff, they all seemed uneasy in answering this question. But when we started dissecting it, they soon realized our company was already the best in the world at what we do. From that day forward they all began to walk with a swagger.

8. **Live your "mission statement" everyday:** "Loomix is dedicated to leading the agricultural community in providing innovation and imagination with its advanced quality controlled products, programs and education, inspired by all to bring safe feed and safe food to the market place". Every employee of our company knows of this mission. This is why they show up for work every day. They sign each letter and email with this statement after their signature. Don't take a chance that your employees do not fully know what is expected of them. Make sure they are clear why they show up for work each day.

9. **Why settle for good when you can have outstanding:** The night my wife told me she wanted to move back to Colorado, I was staying at a large hotel. Anthony Robbins was speaking there. I heard about 20 minutes of his speech but those 20 minutes inspired me immensely. This is what I remember from that night. He said that people who get good results get no rewards, but people who get great results get good rewards, while those that get excellent results get great rewards, and those who get outstanding results get everything. I remember reflecting on my conversation with my wife that night and how she wanted to move back to Colorado. I started reflecting on how I had started out in the lowest ranking position in my company, and now held the position of general manager of the largest company in

my industry. I also remembered how I was thinking, "This is excellent, but is it outstanding?" That night I decided I wanted to be outstanding, and today I have reached that goal. Today, with my partner, I own a company in the same industry and we are the very best in the world at what we do.

10. **Live a balanced life:** Unless you live a balanced life, you will not live an outstanding life. Today my wife of thirty-six years told me she had everything she wanted. She quickly corrected herself and said "we" have everything. She said we have a wonderful family, we have our wonderful Loomix "extended family", we have wonderful material things, we have a great marriage, and we have faith. We don't suffer in any area. During my professional career with this company, we were owned by a privately held family, we were owned by a corporate conglomerate and now we co-own the company. If at any point my personal values were jeopardized it would have destroyed my passion. Over the years they have been tested many times, but through it all, I kept the balance in my life. Often I had to change the setting or change the playing field, but through it all, I kept the same values which drove my success.

Ten Rules for Bootstrapping Your Business
By Thomas Frey, Executive Director, DaVinci Institute
www.DaVinciInstitute.com

While there can never be one perfect way to launch a business, these are some of the practical rules which seem to hold the most truth.

1. **Lead the Life - Cut Your Overhead.** The first rule of boot-strapping is to cut your overhead costs to the bone. To achieve the bootstrapper's mindset, the mental tai chi of becoming singular in your business focus, you must learn to lead the life. Payments for fancy houses and cars will slowly tear away at your personal resolve. Fancy meals at restaurants and lavish parties will compromise your attention. And high-end offices with luxury furnishings will put you at a negotiator's disadvantage.

   Frugality is not a skill that can be turned on and off. It's a concept you must become married to. Every needless penny you spend will jeopardize your ability to succeed.

2. **Never Blame Others – Do It Yourself.** As soon as you find yourself blaming other people for things not being done, just take a deep breath and do it yourself.

   It becomes so easy to let yourself off the hook by simply blaming someone else. But in doing so, you put your company at risk. You have to be the emotional leader driving your business forward, with an unusual level of loyalty for what you're doing. Frustrating as it may seem, you can't expect others to have your same level of drive and commitment. Ultimately, you are singularly accountable for your company's success or failure.

3. **Don't Plan for Failure – Remove the Guardrails at the Cliff.**

Planning for easy bailout options has a way of undermining your resolve. Every startup goes through tumultuous tough times testing the mettle of the entrepreneur. And the tough times are what separate the survivors from the many strewn casualties lying alongside the startup highway.

Planning for failure almost invariably leads to failure. Every step that the early stage entrepreneur takes on the startup tightrope will have them looking for an easier option, a soft landing so to speak. Removing the soft landings has a way of clearing your focus and strengthening your concentration.

4. **Test Your Limits – Constantly.** Expanding skill sets and relentless passion are two key ingredients. But blind passion without the skills can be a very destructive force.

   When is the last time you went outside and physically ran as fast as you possibly can? For most, this was a long time ago. But how will you know how fast you can run if you don't test yourself. This is similar to the business world where knowing your limits is the best way to manage your options.

5. **The Business Plan Fallacy – In Quest of Low Hanging Fruit.** Contrary to what academicians teach, successful bootstrappers seldom write business plans. I've not met many that have. This is a luxury few can afford. But more importantly, bootstrappers have a constant need to keep their options open. Their relentless drive for revenues forces them to keep their peripheral vision intact as they view the opportunity landscape.

   In the early stages of a startup, bootstrappers have little accountability for their actions. Their primary need is to prove a viable concept in a viable market. And this means revenues come before anything else.

6. **The Transitional Business Model - Search for Low Hanging Fruit.** Potential revenue streams come in odd shapes and sizes, but you begin by selling yourself. For that matter, every transaction begins with you selling yourself as a compe-

tent, credible person with great integrity.

Often times the first revenues for a fledgling startup come from individual consulting contracts. Selling your own expertise pays the bills and can set the stage for you to metamorphose into the business you wish to become. Many would-be entrepreneurs fail to think through the options of creating a transitional business model where you begin with an easy entry point and transition into the business you ultimately want to become. This approach will invariably take unexpected twists and turns along the way, so be flexible and know when to make the next turn.

7. **Little Things Matter - Micromanage to Your Advantage.** Sometimes the littlest details will throw your startup company into a tailspin. Blind trust is a luxury that startups can ill afford.

   Understanding your business inside and out will give you much better operational control. In nearly every case there is a direct correlation between the decisions you make and the revenue streams you have coming in. Understanding this cause-and-effect correlation is absolutely critical for you to succeed.

8. **Bankers are not Your Friend - Line up Tons of Credit Before you Start.** Few would-be entrepreneurs can imagine the difficulty of finding credit once they leave their steady income jobs. Credit scoring systems have a way of branding you as a terrible risk almost instantly as you enter the startup starting blocks. So plan ahead and line up credit in whatever forms you can find, and lots of It.

   Business never works the way you have it planned. Chaos theory is alive and well, and will be knocking at your door when you least expect it.

9. **Find a Mentor - Surround Yourself with People Who Look Like What You Want to Become.** Entrepreneurs need to surround themselves with other entrepreneurs. And it's even

better if you can surround yourself with people who are successful in the same type of business you are entering into. Successful people often can't tell you what it is that makes them special, but if you hang around with them, they will teach you through their actions. Sitting in on a negotiating session, or being in the same room when they deal with a personnel issue, will give you unique pieces of information that has never been captured in books.

10. **Reckless and Relentless – The Bootstrapping Difference.** The bootstrapper business model is different than that of a "funded" company. Bootstrapping is more about drive and determination than it is about intelligence, and more about getting things done than doing things right. It's better to get it done than to get it perfect. That's not to say that you shouldn't be bright and try to do things right, but successful bootstrappers tend to be more reckless and driven, and necessarily so, than their 'funded' entrepreneurial counterpart.

APPENDIX C

12 Essential Elements for Entrepreneurial Success
By Dave Block, Cofounder, Make-It-Fly®
www.Make-It-Fly.com

ONE

Passion is paramount.
Entrepreneurs are passionate survivalists. If you aren't passionate about working on your business, it won't survive in the long run. Passion is the imperative ingredient that makes everything else fall into place. It makes surviving the long hours required to run a business possible.

TWO

Make your plan...and then work backwards.
Every entrepreneur needs a plan. Reach into the future and define your goals. Know what you really want in five years, three years and in one year. Then, work backwards to define the key steps that will get you there successfully. What you do now and what you'll do over the next six months will determine where you'll be in two years. It's that simple. By working backwards, you gain a clearer perspective on what your priorities need to be in the present.

THREE

You need to be teachable.
When you're an entrepreneur, "Know-It-Allism" doesn't cut it. Successful entrepreneurs recognize that they're always learning and that they can learn something from everybody. If you aren't willing to truly listen and learn, you'll cheat yourself out of many opportunities.

FOUR

Revere relationships.
Amidst fierce competition in every industry, businesses are driven by relationships—people do business with those they know, like and trust. Each relationship can become a powerful

vortex that spins off more opportunities for both financial and personal growth. Whether you're naturally shy or an extrovert, as an entrepreneur you need to look at building relationships as one of the most effective, efficient and evolutionary components of growing your business.

FIVE

Discover the Power of Weakness.
Entrepreneurs can't be equally effective in all areas of their business. And that's okay! Discovering, understanding and accepting your weaknesses can actually be a gift. They present opportunities because they show you where you need help. Playing the heroic martyr by trying to do it all doesn't grow a company. Paying others to do a job better than you can will.

SIX

Personal Accountability.
As an entrepreneur, no one is there to hold you accountable but yourself. You have to want to be responsible for your actions—whether they're successful or not. When you're in business for yourself, you need to seek out others who'll hold you accountable to do what you committed to. It keeps you honest and moving toward your desired goal.

SEVEN

Be a Business Surgeon.
Successful entrepreneurs must be ruthlessly honest. You need to look at the guts of your business and understand how healthy it is at any given moment. You can't be afraid to look at it for fear of what you may find. Business can be messy, and entrepreneurs have to look at the wounds head-on to heal them quickly and effectively.

EIGHT

Just Ask for Help!
You can't be all things to all people all of the time! Recognize that people love to help people. If you need help, swallow your pride and ask for it. The relief you'll experience will far outweigh the discomfort of admitting you need assistance. Plus you'll have the added bonus of allowing another person the good feelings

associated with pitching in. So don't be afraid to ask for help!

NINE
Evaluate. Evaluate. Evaluate.
As an entrepreneur, you have to track your progress every step of the way. Evaluating and discovering what doesn't work is just as important if not more so than knowing what works. But you must have measurable indicators upon which to base your evaluations. If you don't, how do you really know if you're on track or way off course?

TEN
Pursue a Balanced Life.
Entrepreneurship can be an all-consuming endeavor, yet it's critical to maintain balance in your life. Small-business owners tend to get so engrossed in their business that their personal life suffers. But by being just as committed to the health of your personal life as you are to your business, your business will thrive.

ELEVEN
Don't Be Technologically Timid.
Whether you love it or hate it, you should embrace technology in business. Technology can make your ability to effectively communicate soar. Discard your fears of technical communication and take advantage of technology to improve your business wherever you can.

TWELVE
Be Well Advised.
Every entrepreneur should have his or her own advisory board. Witness the amazing power when many business owners, in the same room at the same time, focus on your business.

"Until one is committed, there is hesitancy, the chance to draw back, always ineffectiveness. Concerning all acts of initiative there is one elementary truth, the ignorance of which kills countless ideas and splendid plans: that the moment one definitely commits oneself, then providence moves too. All sorts of things occur to help one that would never otherwise have occurred. A whole stream of events issues from the decision, raising in one's favor all man-ner of unforeseen incidents and meetings and material assistance, which no man could have dreamed would have come his way."

-William H. Murray

35 Keys to Business Success
By Jake Jabs
American Furniture Warehouse
www.jakejabs.com

These principles are key to business success. Remarkable men have coined some of these phrases. But more than that, they've lived by them. Adopt these thoughts daily and you're bound to net the rewards you seek.

1. Fulfill a demand and you will be successful.
2. Be honest and you will never have to worry about what you said before.
3. Give value and service.
4. Live below your means.
5. Don't go into business just to make money.
6. Don't be afraid to sell cheap, have the best prices in town.
7. Business must have a value to society and not just a profit machine for the family.
8. Believe in the free enterprise system.
9. Believe the United States is the land of opportunity.
10. Believe we are living in the greatest time in the history of the world.
11. Get an education. This develops confidence and opens doors.
12. Develop an art form and hobbies. These will help you through the trouble times.
13. Develop confidence in yourself. Organize your time, make a list and move priorities to the top.
14. Keep physically fit, it helps your mental attitude.
15. Worry not about tomorrow because tomorrow will take care of itself.
16. It's ok to be a work-a-holic. Hard work is good for you. It can be therapeutic.
17. Challenge yourself.

18.   Be a risk taker.
19.   Learn to say no.
20.   Enthusiasm will always be contagious.
21.   To achieve success you must swallow your ego. Ego trips can break you.
22.   If you enjoy what you are doing you may never have to work a day in your life.
23.   A successful person is one who does the task nobody else will do.
24.   Keep your house in order.
25.   To succeed you have to be willing to fail.
26.   A great man is one who can walk with the common man but talk with kings.
27.   Success is achieving what is important to you.
28.   Be a good steward with what God has given you.
29.   Don't love money. The love of money is the root of all evil.
30.   Talk health, happiness and prosperity to every person you meet.
31.   Ask not what your country can do for you, but what you can do for your country.
32.   Competition is the spice of life. If forces lower prices and gives more value.
33.   Small business-entrepreneurship is the lifeblood of America.
34.   We must teach free enterprise, free market, entrepreneurship and capitalism in our schools.
35.   Get involved in your community.

These 35 key thoughts are an excerpt from Jake's autobiography he wrote in 2000. If you'd like to pick up a copy of his book, call or visit any American Furniture Warehouse store.

The 5 Essential Skills Needed to Create a Great Business

By Erin Duckhorn of E-Myth Worldwide
www.e-myth.com

In Michael Gerber's book, The Power Point, he states that there are five essential skills every entrepreneur must have in order to create a great business. Consciously or unconsciously, every entrepreneur does these things to some extent in their business. But it's the ones who master these skills that will create world-class businesses.

1. Concentration. The inner force and energy that allows you to focus your attention. This is the foundation for everything — without the ability to focus, you cannot live on purpose. If you have three projects on your desk and you work on all of them at once, you're not likely to get anything done. Not to mention the fact that when you spread your attention too thin, you're just not capable of doing your best work. Concentration allows you to focus with laser precision on that which needs to be done.

2. Discrimination. The ability to choose upon what, where and who our attention (or concentration) is directed. It's through discrimination that a business develops standards and discipline. Discrimination is about picking and choosing your battles. It's about prioritizing. It's about choosing to work on the things that will deliver the biggest return for your efforts. We've worked with tens of thousands of clients, and this is the skill that often trips people up. When you're bogged down in the day-to-day activities of running a business, prioritizing can be a struggle. The programs offered by E-Myth Worldwide include worksheets and tools to help you create systems that allow you to discriminate the work you should be doing: prioritizing around that which will give you the greatest return for your efforts.

3. Organization. This is the ability to turn chaos into order. Once you're able to concentrate and discriminate you need to create order and predictability so you can successfully grow your business. This involves the creation of systems that allow your business to run efficiently.

4. Innovation. Once you've begun to hone your focus on the right things, and you've achieved some order to your world, you can begin to innovate. Innovation is part of the Business Development Cycle. Innovation is that spark of genius that all entrepreneurs have, and should be seen as an asset. An asset that can be leveraged for the greater good of the entire organization. An asset that will add business value over time. Lots of us have ideas, but when you've developed the skill of innovation, you're able to take that moment of inspiration and capture it, recreate it, and most importantly take action on it.

5. Communication. The ability to transmit ideas with clarity, precision, passion and purpose. People want to be inspired and part of something important. You must communicate your passion, your vision and your ideas to your employees, your customers your lenders, your vendors — everyone who is touched by your business. Concentration provides the energy and attention needed for action, discrimination provides the intention and standards to know what action needs to be taken, organization provides the room for right action to take place, innovation spurs new ideas and communication is the channel through which the ultimate vision is realized.

Sixteen Rules

By Bob Parsons, CEO of The Go Daddy Group
www.bobparsons.com

1. Get and stay out of your comfort zone. I believe that not much happens of any significance when we're in our comfort zone. I hear people say, "But I'm concerned about security." My response to that is simple: "Security is for cadavers."

2. Never give up. Almost nothing works the first time it's attempted. Just because what you're doing does not seem to be working, doesn't mean it won't work. It just means that it might not work the way you're doing it. If it was easy, everyone would be doing it, and you wouldn't have an opportunity.

3. When you're ready to quit, you're closer than you think. There's an old Chinese saying that I just love, and I believe it is so true. It goes like this: "The temptation to quit will be greatest just before you are about to succeed."

4. With regard to whatever worries you, not only accept the worst thing that could happen, but make it a point to quantify what the worst thing could be. Very seldom will the worst consequence be anywhere near as bad as a cloud of "undefined consequences." My father would tell me early on, when I was struggling and losing my shirt trying to get Parsons Technology going, "Well, Robert, if it doesn't work, they can't eat you."

5. Focus on what you want to have happen. Remember that old saying, "As you think, so shall you be."

6. Take things a day at a time. No matter how difficult your situation is, you can get through it if you don't look too far into the future, and focus on the present moment. You can get through anything one day at a time.

7. Always be moving forward. Never stop investing. Never stop improving. Never stop doing something new. The moment you stop improving your organization, it starts to die. Make it your goal to be better each and every day, in some small way. Remember the Japanese concept of Kaizen. Small daily improvements eventually result in huge advantages.

8. Be quick to decide. Remember what General George S. Patton said: "A good plan violently executed today is far and away better than a perfect plan tomorrow."

9. Measure everything of significance. I swear this is true. Anything that is measured and watched, improves.

10. Anything that is not managed will deteriorate. If you want to uncover problems you don't know about, take a few moments and look closely at the areas you haven't examined for a while. I guarantee you problems will be there.

11. Pay attention to your competitors, but pay more attention to what you're doing. When you look at your competitors, remember that everything looks perfect at a distance. Even the planet Earth, if you get far enough into space, looks like a peaceful place.

12. Never let anybody push you around. In our society, with our laws and even playing field, you have just as much right to what you're doing as anyone else, provided that what you're doing is legal.

13. Never expect life to be fair. Life isn't fair. You make your own breaks. You'll be doing good if the only meaning fair has to you, is something that you pay when you get on a bus (i.e., fare).

14. Solve your own problems. You'll find that by coming up with your own solutions, you'll develop a competitive edge. Masura Ibuka, the co-founder of SONY, said it best: "You never succeed in technology, business, or anything by following the others." There's also an old Asian saying that I remind myself of frequently. It goes like this: "A wise man keeps his own counsel."

15. Don't take yourself too seriously. Lighten up. Often, at least half of what we accomplish is due to luck. None of us are in control as much as we like to think we are.

16. There's always a reason to smile. Find it. After all, you're really lucky just to be alive. Life is short. More and more, I agree with my little brother. He always reminds me: "We're not here for a long time; we're here for a good time."

These sixteen rules are included with the permission of Bob Parsons (http://www.bobparsons.com) and is Copyright ©2004-2006 by Bob Parsons. All rights reserved.

ABOUT THE AUTHOR

Brian Schwartz grew up in Northern California and attended college in San Luis Obispo graduating with a Bachelor of Arts degree in Industrial Technology in 1994. Over a span of thirteen years, he worked for a half a dozen technology startups and large corporations moving around the country to advance his career. Living through many acquisitions, layoffs, and no fewer than ten different managers along the way, life had lost meaning to him. What remained was a general feeling of dissatisfaction and lack of fulfillment. In 2007, while seeking answers, he discovered a transformational course that served as the catalyst he needed for change. What he learned that weekend was what he had thought were his personal values and priorities, were, in fact, those of others. He began to reinvent himself and live a life more aligned with his true self making positive changes including quitting his high stress six figure job. Through this project, he discovered that the right questions bring amazing clarity to life when we seek our own answers and that as our own truth emerges, we discover we are more powerful than we realized. Brian's new found passion is to inspire others to realize that we each have a unique ability to make an impact in the world, and we owe it to ourselves and the world to follow our inspired thoughts through to action. Brian currently lives in Northern Colorado with his wife Debi.

Brian is also a passionate speaker and workshop facilitator, and open to just about anything else he can do to help others adopt the *50 Interviews*™ framework for themselves.

Brian Is currently seeking 'correspondents' to further expand the 50 Interviews™ series. To learn how you can get involved visit www.50interviews.com. He can be reached via email at: 50Interviews@gmail.com.

LETTER TO THE READER

Dear Reader,

I truly appreciate you purchasing this book. Because I'm grateful to you, I wanted to share something that extends beyond these pages.

I invite you to check out the online companion at:

www.50interviews.com/join

After you register, a password will be emailed to you granting you access to a vast amount of companion content, including:

- Additional interviews.
- Opportunities to connect with the people interviewed in the book.
- Audio and video downloads of entire interviews.
- News on the upcoming video companion at www.50interviews.tv
- Hundreds of related online resources
- All the recommended books mentioned throughout the interviews compiled in a single guide.
- Lists of questions to consider as you begin doing your own interviews.
- How you can personally get involved in a future volume of *50 Interviews*!

We plan to add more resources, helpful articles, and pull in a lot of material that was shared with us during the interviews.

To your success and all the best,

Brian Schwartz